"While reading *Delight in Your Child's Design,* I yelled two things out loud (much to the surprise of the airline passengers seated near me): "I love Kristen, Ricky Neal, and Patrick more than I did fifteen minutes ago" and "I wish I would have written this book." You'll be doing the Happy Reader Dance with me as you dive into Laurie Winslow Sargent's charming writing style and discover scads of practical take-away suggestions for appreciating and encouraging the one-of-a-kind temperaments of your children. *Delight in Your Child's Design* is an incredible resource for parents; it is now number one on my list of recommended reading, both professionally and as a mom who loves to pass along a great read."

JULIE ANN BARNHILL
Speaker and author of *She's Gonna Blow!*

"Laurie Sargent's refreshing new book, *Delight in Your Child's Design,* will help parents enjoy each stage of their children's lives, enable them to appreciate how God has uniquely designed their kids, and equip them to nurture their children with love and acceptance."

CHERI FULLER
Speaker and author of *The Mom You're Meant to Be*
and the School Saavy Kids series

"This is a great book. I highly recommend it and wish it were on the must-read list for every parent."

PATRICIA H. RUSHFORD
Author of *What Kids Need Most in a Mom*
and *It Shouldn't Hurt to Be a Kid*

D0107142

"I see it in my work all the time. Parents want their child to be a unique individual, but then others pressure them to "mold" the uniqueness right out of their child! Laurie's commonsense approach reminds us what we as parents and teachers intrinsically know but sometimes fail to do—celebrate each child's unique personality as a true gift."

SALLY SMITH
Director, Best Beginnings Preschool
Redmond, Washington

"Laurie Sargent genuinely celebrates the strengths and differences in children, and offers so many practical ways for discovering what works. Every parent can find hope, encouragement, and hands-on strategies in *Delight in Your Child's Design*—it's a great resource!"

CYNTHIA TOBIAS
Author of *The Way They Learn*

"In the middle of feeding, disciplining, refereeing, and taxiing our children, we sometimes forget to enjoy them. I am so thankful to Laurie Winslow Sargent for reminding us to make cherishing our children's uniqueness a focused priority in *Delight in Your Child's Design*."

LISA WHELCHEL
Author of *Creative Correction* and *The Facts of Life and Other Lessons My Father Taught Me*

DELIGHT IN YOUR CHILD'S DESIGN

DELIGHT

IN YOUR

CHILD'S

DESIGN

LAURIE WINSLOW
SARGENT

Tyndale House
Publishers, Inc.
WHEATON, ILLINOIS

Visit Tyndale's exciting Web site at www.tyndale.com

Copyright © 2005 by Laurie Winslow Sargent. All rights reserved.

TYNDALE is a registered trademark of Tyndale House Publishers, Inc.

Tyndale's quill logo is a trademark of Tyndale House Publishers, Inc.

Focus on the Family is a registered trademark of Focus on the Family, Colorado Springs, Colorado.

Cover photo copyright © by Alamy.com. All rights reserved.

Author photo copyright © 2002 by Yuen Lui Studio, Inc. All rights reserved.

Designed by Ron Kaufmann

Published in association with the literary agency of Alive Communications, Inc., 7680 Goddard Street, Suite 200, Colorado Springs, CO 80920.

Library of Congress Cataloging-in-Publication Data

Sargent, Laurie Winslow.
  Delight in your child's design : how to better understand, nurture, and enjoy your child's unique traits and temperament / Laurie Winslow Sargent.
    p. cm.
  ISBN 0-8423-7130-3
    1. Temperament in children. 2. Personality in children. 3. Temperament—Religious aspects—Christianity. 4. Parent and child—Religious aspects—Christianity. I. Title.
  BF723. T53S27 2005
  248.8'45—dc22   2004026287

Printed in the United States of America

11 10 09 08 07 06 05
 7   6   5   4   3   2   1

To my incredible children: Tyler, Aimee, and Elisa.
I delight thoroughly in the way each of you is designed!

Special thanks to:
My Lord and Savior, Jesus Christ,
who greatly impacts my attitude toward children
and convinces me that every child is precious and unique.

CONTENTS

INTRODUCTION
Choosing the Child You've Been Given xiii

1
DELIGHTED OR DISILLUSIONED? 1
Assess why parenting may not be as delightful as you'd hoped, while recognizing that it is possible to feel increased delight in your kids.

2
TOUGH STUFF 17
Discover how your own schedule, health, or past experiences may block delight, and learn how to find support.

3
FROM DNA TO BIRTH DAY 37
Consider some fascinating facts about your child's complexity, from conception to birth.

4
PERSONALITY POTLUCK 51
Realize how your child's God-given personality differences make her one-of-a-kind!

5

CLASH AND BURN 73

Explore why and how personality conflicts provoke anger and impatience so you can learn how to better relate to your child.

6

DISABILITY DILEMMAS 89

Consider when to suspect a disability, where to find help if you are concerned, and how to help your child if he does have special challenges.

7

LOVE IS A VERB 107

Express renewed delight through the attitudes and actions most meaningful to your child.

NOTES 133

APPENDIX A

Parenting Resources 137
Parenting Groups 141

APPENDIX B

Special Challenges of the Specially Gifted 143

ACKNOWLEDGEMENTS

Thanks to Mama (Jillian Pearce Winslow), whose encouraging words and faith in my abilities helped show me how to appreciate my own children.

Thanks, with kisses, to my dear hubby, Gordy, for eating too much fast food and taking the kids on countless hikes so I could get this book done. Thanks, too, for modeling delight in our children: you express that so creatively to them. You help me keep my perspective on days when parenting is not as delightful as it should be.

Thanks to my amazing editor, Kim Miller, whose sensitivity and great insights did so much to help shape this book. She also contributed the "Your Child's Got Personality!" sidebar in chapter 4.

Thanks to my inspiring, praying, and hands-on helpful critique group members: Judy Bodmer, Thornton (Thorn) Ford, Martin (Marty) Nystrom, Paul Malm, and Roberta (Peg) Kehle, and this book's first readers, including Mary Vermeulen and the Reidt family. Every writer needs to hear "We love your stories!" balanced with "This section needs work. Have you thought of . . . ?" I also deeply appreciate the people whose letters and stories I use within these pages. Your honesty will help so many other parents learn how to delight more in their children.

Thanks also to all my friends at Northwest Christian Writers Association (NCWA) and the Advanced Writers and Speakers Association (AWSA).

INTRODUCTION

Choosing the Child You've Been Given

Remember the first time your baby smiled at you? Eyes fixed on you, arms waving with excitement, your little one rewarded your months of selfless nurturing and sleep deprivation with a toothless grin. At that moment, delighting in him or her probably felt like the most natural and uncomplicated reaction in the world.

But how about yesterday or today—now that your baby is a toddler, or a kindergartner, or a sixth grader? When did you last consciously think: *Isn't she wonderful?* or *What a gift he is to me!?*

Traffic jams, work deadlines, sibling squabbles, grocery lines—even the urge to hurry kids into bed so you'll have a few minutes to yourself—all can dampen delight. Busy schedules or lack of sleep may keep you from stopping, looking, and listening to your kids long enough to appreciate them fully. Also, sometimes your children's personality traits, learning styles, or disabilities may baffle, frustrate, irritate, or worry you . . . distracting you from what is worthy of appreciation.

You may have a child going through a "stage": defiantly attempting to exert his or her independence. (And for some children, those stages never seem to end.) Children with strong-willed personalities or severe behavioral difficulties often create conflicts that snuff out feelings of delight and generate impatience and anger instead. But even moms and dads with "good" kids discover that parenting has its ups and downs, as kids test limits or ride emotional roller coasters.

I've experienced those ups and downs firsthand, yet children delight me. I never cease to be amazed at how imaginative, hilarious, interesting, and compassionate they can be. My life is richer especially because of my own three children, now ages eight, fourteen, and eighteen. I've observed and cherished many other children as well.

My fascination with children began during my training and then five years of work in the field of occupational therapy. It has continued during the eighteen years my husband, Gordon, and I have been raising our kids. I've gained insight from countless discussions with moms in parent support groups and during my years as a crisis counselor. I also have learned from the responses of readers of my magazine articles and my book *The Power of Parent-Child Play* and from those who have responded to my live radio interviews. It's become apparent to me that parents across the globe long to connect more meaningfully with their kids and reap more joy from parenting. Some of the e-mails I've received through my Web site testify to this longing.

Heather Ann told me that she enjoys being a mom—yet admitted that she "felt very 'far away'" from her five-year-old son. Pamela, who lives in the Philippines, wrote about her experiences with her daughter, almost four, and son, nearly two. She left her nursing career when her daughter was born and admitted, "There are days when I wonder if I am contributing anything significant to this world." Sharleen, a Canadian who has two adult children and two younger kids, said that although she knew her children were quite different, "I was trying to fit them into a certain personality-type mold." She wasn't satisfied with the results. Perhaps you can identify with Heather Ann, Pamela, or Sharleen—or perhaps you sometimes struggle to delight in your kids for a different reason.

My desire is to put an arm around parents and offer a compassionate ear to those who aren't feeling as much delight as possible. I want to acknowledge difficulties while also extending hope for joy in intimate parent-child relationships. I want to inspire moms and dads to express their love for their children in new or consistent ways.

God gave you no higher calling than to raise your kids, but like any other great challenge, it is as likely to produce frustration as joy. Or time may trickle away like sand through your fingers, each grain a lost opportunity to connect with your child. That three-year-old with monsters under his bed will suddenly be a young man needing extralong sheets for his college-dorm bed, under which mere dust bunnies will reside.

So what's the solution? Must we simply choose to be cheerful? If the power of positive thinking were all you needed, I'd turn you over to Norman Vincent Peale. But there are concrete things you can do to enhance your delight in your children—tools to help you better:

- **Know your child**: Even before birth, kids are amazingly complex. I'll explain how you can discover your child's unique personality traits and abilities. Learning to delight will require some deliberate exploration into what makes your child tick, to seek—as if on a treasure hunt—what is remarkable about him, and to rejoice when you find it. I firmly believe that once you realize how truly amazing your child is, new attitudes and actions will come from deep within you—actions that are likely to impact your child for life.
- **Live with your child**: We'll discuss how to deal positively with differences that can make life difficult (or intriguing!) and talk about the pros and cons of labeling.
- **Delight in your child**: I'll offer new and creative ways to express your love and appreciation to your child.
- **Know yourself**: Along the way, I'll help you explore what may keep you from enjoying your kids—and perhaps life—as much as possible. And ideally, you will find more joy in your role as a parent.

You are not destined to merely raise your child. You have an exclusive opportunity to get to know a one-of-a-kind human being. Your child has thoughts and feelings like no other: inborn, God-given traits and potential that you have the privilege and honor of nurturing. This means you are tremendously valuable—an unparalleled gift to your child.

As you get to know your child more intimately, I believe you'll become more patient, compassionate, and wise in the way you parent. And as you find more creative ways to express your appreciation, your child will flourish and your relationship will be enriched.

So let the adventure begin!

1

DELIGHTED OR DISILLUSIONED?

Delight
1. A high degree of gratification;
2. A sense of great satisfaction;
3. Keen enjoyment;
4. Lively pleasure;
5. Joy[1]

Mom, can't we *please* go to the park?" seven-year-old Elisa asked as she pulled on my arm.

Arghh. I'd just settled—finally—into the recliner for a little coffee break after working all afternoon at my in-home office. *I'll get so cold standing on that playground watching her! Do I have to?* I thought.

"Are you sure you wouldn't rather cuddle and read a story?" I asked.

"Aww, c'mon, Mom. I want to swing on the monkey bars."

Sigh. "Okay," I said, struggling to hide my exasperation. I knew she simply had to get outside to do something active or she'd beg me all evening to take her out. It was simply the way she was wired. *Chalk up one more to the sacrifices of mother-hood.* I got our coats.

At the park, I impatiently shifted my feet back and forth. I blew out my white breath. I clapped my gloves together to keep warm. "Just ten more minutes!" I called out, as Elisa shimmied up a pole to some very high bars.

She swung powerfully, back and forth, back and forth. Startled out of my discomfort and impatience, I marveled at her coordination, and not for the first time.

"Wow, that's great!" I cried out. *I never could have done that as a kid—nor would I have even wanted to! What makes her that way? She obviously didn't inherit the klutz gene from me.*

While Elisa played, I thought about how she'd always used her whole body to express her personality. She never walked downstairs, she leapt—four steps at a time. She was compelled to get in her quota of at least 1,642 cartwheels per day. I wondered, *When was it that she first earned the nickname Monkey?*

Perhaps it was when, at age two and a half, she declared she'd climb the rock wall at the outdoor store REI (and did so a few short years later). Or perhaps it was the day when she was only sixteen months old when, horrified, I spotted her crawling across the top of the monkey bars on our backyard swing set. As I ran to save her, she nonchalantly climbed back down! Hmm. Or was she already our Monkey at a mere three months, incessantly standing on our laps as we held her? I wondered, *If she could have grabbed my rib cage before she was born, would she have swung from that? What makes her so nimble and so adventurous?*

Suddenly I realized we had to scoot to make it to Costco before the store closed. Elisa and I left the park, picked up her big sister, Aimee, and I fought traffic as the kids bickered in the backseat.

"Stop that!" I said.

"It's *her* fault!" they chorused.

"It takes *two* to make a fight!" I replied *very* loudly and impatiently. (And that made three.)

As we entered the warehouse, Elisa's face lit up at the sight of those wonderfully wide, long aisles. She impulsively cartwheeled through the office-supply section. I cried, "Look out!" as her foot nearly connected with a customer's chin. I apologized, embarrassed. Frustration mounted as I approached the long checkout lines.

Later that evening, I guiltily looked forward to a quiet house with kids nestled in their beds. But my first request to "Get on your pj's and brush your teeth now" fell on deaf ears, as Elisa attempted some last-minute acrobatics.

"Okay, okay," I grumbled, "just three more somersaults down the hall and *that's it*–uh-oh! Watch the lamp!" *So much for the trip to the park to help release her energy.*

Eventually, Elisa's sweet, high voice called from down the hall, "Mommy, Daddy, tuck-in!" We went into her room and bent over for the obligatory chain of butterfly kisses, fishy kisses, and Eskimo kisses. But as I nuzzled her soft face, I was drawn in. I lingered. My little pixie grinned charmingly–minus a few teeth the tooth fairy had taken–and sighed, "You're the *best* mom in the whole wide world!"

Hardly, I thought. Yet my heart lifted. A grin tugged at the corners of my mouth as I recalled Costco cartwheels, somer-saults down the hall . . . and her enthusiasm for life and tenderness toward me. My weariness from caring for an energetic child was replaced by delight in her and the privilege of being her mother. *I'm so glad I'm her mom,* I thought as I switched off the light. I couldn't wait to tuck in Aimee next!

TOO BUSY, TOO TIRED, TOO IMPATIENT, TOO DISTRACTED?

In the course of a single day, parenting offers up an emotional smorgasbord: Exhaustion. Pride. Impatience. Delight for dessert—yet we can be too full of other emotions to make room for joy. That's because while we love our children, so much can interfere with our *truly* enjoying them.

In a single moment you may experience a double whammy: exhaustion from work (whether that means back-to-back business meetings or eight loads of laundry) while dealing with a chronically arguing child whose extremely high energy level and distractibility also frustrate you. Instead of marveling at the wonder of your child's being, you may wonder if you'll keep your sanity!

WHILE WE LOVE OUR CHILDREN, SO MUCH CAN INTERFERE WITH OUR *TRULY* ENJOYING THEM.

On good days, if you're dealing with a child who has energy to burn and an art for endless negotiation, you may be future-thinking enough to realize that he may *someday* become a dynamic salesman or lawyer. You may even joke about your desire to bottle and sell his energy. But often you simply and frankly admit, "He's a handful!" You may think, *I do love this child, but I don't like him very much today!* Or *I do love him. But caring for him is wearing me down, physically and emotionally.*

I think every parent feels like that on some days. But if those feelings are chronic, it's definitely time for a more joyful, optimistic attitude.

WHY DELIGHT?

Why—with all the other things we must focus on as parents—is it so important to learn to delight more in our kids? Do our feelings really matter as long as we get the job done?

Yes! As your delight in your child increases (I'll soon explain *how*), you both will experience many benefits:

· **Your child will be assured of one place he can count on being accepted and loved.** Your home can be a place of refuge, where your child's self-confidence and optimism are continually recharged. Remember the children's book character Alexander and his terrible, horrible, no good, very bad day? From discovering gum in his hair when he wakes up, to being deserted by his best friend, to learning that he has a cavity during his dentist appointment, the seven-year-old laments a day that goes from bad to worse. In fact, he repeatedly wishes he could move to Australia. Maybe a horrible day here would be a wonderful one there![2]

In truth, bad days aren't so easy for our kids to escape. They regularly need reassurance that they are valued and can overcome difficulties that come their way: put-downs from a bully, sour looks from a teacher . . . perhaps even more difficult crises that we hope our children will never have to endure. Consider your delight in your child an inoculation against despair. While not providing full immunity—life will always have its challenges—a child who feels unconditional love will be more resilient, self-confident, and hopeful.

For years, my son's friend Cameron too often slept on other people's couches or had the extra plate at someone else's dinner table. When he was staying at our house, he quietly observed my husband, Gordy, and I show playful affection to each other and our kids. Sometimes he laughed. Sometimes we saw pain in his eyes and realized it was hard for him to watch. We knew his single-parent dad did not seem able to meet his physical or emotional needs.

CONSIDER YOUR DELIGHT IN YOUR CHILD AN INOCULATION AGAINST DESPAIR.

When it became apparent that Cameron desperately needed an accepting, loving home of his own, his mother, Donna—with her five-year-old daughter—bravely boarded the train in Georgia to move to Washington state and regain custody of her son. At first, living out of suitcases in my home office with her confused little daughter, Imani, proved overwhelming for Donna. She didn't have a job that could adequately support a single mom of two. And Cameron, for whom she'd moved out West in the first place, was hesitant to open his heart to her because he'd been hurt so many times.

Then in God's perfect timing, Donna found confirmation she'd made the right decision in a poem her son had written before he knew she was coming to Washington. We wept at his poignant words:

No one to tuck me in at night
No one to say, "Don't let the bugs bite"
No one to say "I'm proud of you"
No one to say "I love you."

Never underestimate the power of family, silly bedtime rituals, or your child's having his own place at the dinner table. But remember too the power in those words: "I'm proud of you"; "I love you."

· **The more you enjoy and appreciate your child, the more pleasurable life will be for you.** I have a beautiful set of twelve nesting gift boxes that have been not only used and reused for gift giving, but also repeatedly stacked, tumbled, and renested by my kids. There's a fascination in removing one box at a time, from the largest to the smallest. After all, the center box, the tiniest one of all—about an inch square—could hold the greatest treasure, even a glittering diamond.

The fresh surprise and delight felt as each smaller box is revealed, in anticipation of what will be found next, can be experienced when you take time to "unpack" your child. Can you see beyond his superficial wrappings: his physical appearance and behavior?

Peel away the stereotypical thinking, and you'll discover his personal learning style and motivations. And eventually, with enough loving, deliberate intent, you're likely to uncover what's at the center of your child, what makes her a real treasure: her soul, spirit, and unique thoughts and feelings. It's *then* that you'll see your child more fully as a gift, not just a responsibility.

Not only can you enjoy and appreciate what makes your child unique, you can find much humor in parenting. Kids can be so very *funny*—often not intentionally so, yet funny nonetheless. The way a toddler waddles like a duck makes us giggle, while at the same time we're bursting with pride at his new accomplishment. A preschooler mutilates a sentence or new word because he doesn't quite hear it right, and we laugh—not in derision, but because his interpretation is not so far off. In a sense we laugh at our own language.

Once my son, then a preschooler, excitedly returned from the county fair to tell me he'd gotten an ink stamp on his "knifehead."

"Your what?" I asked.

He lifted his bangs and gestured, and I said, "You mean, your *fore*head?"

"Oh yeah!" he brightly answered, "my *fork*head!"

Enjoying your child's attributes and funny comments is good for you. Proverbs 17:22 tells us that a cheerful heart is "good medicine" but "a crushed spirit dries up the bones." Have you ever thought of joy in your children as a healing influence? as an energy producer instead of an energy reducer?

· **A child who knows how it feels to be appreciated is more likely to encourage others.** I saw Elisa, a first grader, put this into action recently. As she sat quietly in the church pew next to me, she spontaneously scribbled a note to our pastor, telling him she *loved* his speeches (especially the stories Pastor Jim weaves into his sermons). After the worship service, she insisted on taking her note to him.

Later I wondered, *Did any of the other thousand people attending that service—or any of the five thousand there that weekend—think to encourage him that day?* I also wondered, *How many of the people who clamored around Jesus, as He told His clever parables, thought to tell Him, "We love Your speeches!"?*

If any did, they might well have been children. To this day children respond to Jesus' stories, and even a very small child grasps the importance of the shepherd who rejoiced at finding his lost sheep.[3]

I also wonder if Jesus found it rejuvenating to hold precious, smiling, loose-toothed children, bursting with eager questions, open hearts, and funny mispronunciations? On one occasion, His disciples attempted to shoo some children away, seeming to think they should be seen but not heard in the Master's presence.[4] Jesus, instead, welcomed them into His open arms. He taught the grown-ups that they needed to become more like those children.

As Christ revealed His love for children, those little boys and girls must have responded with eager affection, which I imagine in turn warmed Jesus' heart.

My daughter Elisa's encouraging words to our pastor came from deep within her, without prompting. Her sister, Aimee, often writes words of affirmation to others. (I save many of her little notes to me to reread when I need a boost!) Yet those words were much like those my children have heard from each other, Mom and Dad, and others.

Appreciation is like a boomerang. Delight in your children, and it will eventually circle around back to you.

· **A child who feels valued responds more positively to discipline and guidance.** Your child senses it when you delight in him. The attitude of your heart is reflected in your words and actions, from a simple, brief adoring look to a warmly spoken "I love you!"

But, oddly enough, delighting in your child does not mean you will always make him happy. Other words and actions that *stem* from delight in your child may actually infuriate him, when that means saying NO to something he wants to do.

Yet to stand firm—with energy and commitment—requires unwavering belief in your child's value and potential. In other words, it communicates true delight in him. Cameron had additional lines in his poem, which we as parents can all learn from. He wrote of enjoying freedom to come and go as he pleased, yet he included these words of longing: "No one to say, 'Be home by midnight.'"

Valuing your child also means understanding your child well enough to know what is likely to trigger inappropriate behavior. That can help you be more patient in the midst of conflicts and think more creatively about how to motivate

APPRECIATION IS LIKE A BOOMERANG. DELIGHT IN YOUR CHILDREN, AND IT WILL EVENTUALLY CIRCLE AROUND BACK TO YOU.

positive behavior. For example, three kids will react differently to the common disciplinary measure of time-out.

One child sees a time-out as a positive break from tension. He doesn't like being sent to his room, but after a short bout of crying he'll begin quietly playing with his toys. Whether he knows it or not, he needs time alone to calm down.

Another child can't stand to be away from people for more than five minutes. Time-out means torture. She quickly begs for mercy, forgiveness—whatever it takes to get out of solitary confinement.

For a third child, a time-out is just an enormous battle of wills. Though he doesn't like being confined to his room, he may smugly refuse to come out . . . that is, until Mom does the begging. Or, like my son, he may try to find a way around his confinement. I recall sending toddler Tyler to a time-out in a kid-sized chair, telling him in a serious voice, "I don't want to see your bottom out of that chair for five minutes." A minute or so later he walked into the room with a wide grin, holding the seat of his chair firmly to his bottom!

Kids react differently to disciplinary measures because *what is important to them varies.* One craves solitude; another, people; yet another desires control and leadership. The good news is that what drives children can motivate them to change difficult behavior. Delighting in your child will come more naturally as you understand her priorities and feelings, despite argumentative moments. And sensing your delight, she'll eventually be more open to correction.

· **Your appreciation of your child is likely to impact him for life!** The inventor Thomas Alva Edison was labeled "addled" by his teachers and was kicked out of public school at a young age. Thankfully, his family saw his potential and nurtured it. His mother homeschooled him for a while, which gave him tinkering time, access to advanced text-books, and a basement laboratory. By age twelve he was a successful entrepreneur. Addled? Not quite!

Edison eventually wrote this unforgettable tribute to his mother:

> If it had not been for her *appreciation and faith in me* at a critical time in my experience, I should never likely have become an inventor. I was always a care-less boy, and with a mother of different mental caliber, I should have turned out badly. But her firmness, her sweetness, her goodness were potent powers to keep me in the right path. My mother was the making of me. She was so true, so sure of me . . .[5] (italics mine).

Is it actually possible that without the encouragement of Edison's mother, we might not have had the phonograph or the incandescent lightbulb, or his many other inven-tions? Or would Edison's innate personality and gifts have led him, no matter what, to be an inventor?

Certainly his parents and sister had an impact as they recognized and nurtured his interests and talents, stood up for him, and believed in his abilities and potential.

At age two, Edison (then called "Little Al") was found

sitting in the barn on a goose egg, trying to hatch it. His big sister's husband, Homer, laughed and called him a little goose for trying it. But Al's sister, Marion, soothed his hurt feelings by saying, "It's all right, Al, you did a very smart thing even if it didn't work. If no one ever tried anything, even what some folks say is impossible, no one would learn anything. *So you just keep on trying and maybe some day you'll try something that will work."*[6]

Marion no doubt had heard encouraging words from their mother as well. She knew just the right thing to say to her little brother—even though she probably never imagined that he'd someday be a famous inventor. (Incidentally, more than one thousand patents were issued to Edison.)

We must balance our sense of appreciation of the inborn abilities of a child with recognition that we, as parents, do make a difference. Your supportive parenting may affect your daughter's choice of a spouse who will also love and honor her. It may affect your son's confidence in his choice of a career. And it will ultimately affect the way your children parent their own kids.

WHY NOT DELIGHT?

Part of learning to delight is getting to know your child better. In this book, you'll explore the attributes and characteristics that make your child unique, fascinating, and sometimes difficult to live with.

First, we'll consider the recipe for your child's genetic makeup, which began shaping him long before birth. My nephew Jared was smaller than a grain of rice when it was already determined that he'd have red hair like his uncle Frank.

"I am fearfully and wonderfully made," said the psalmist (139:14). I think you'll get a fresh appreciation of your child as you consider that God has given him his unique identity. We can learn much from science about the complexity of humans and how early your child was destined to have his distinct physical traits. Next, you'll be invited to consider the personality style of your child. A simple assessment of your kid's personality traits and abilities can go a long way in helping identify not only his or her weak areas, but strengths you can rejoice in and express appreciation for. Then I'll speak honestly about the personality clashes between parents and children and offer practical ways to avoid unnecessary conflict.

But wait, you may be thinking, *my child is so complicated, so hard to understand.*

How well I know it! I remember frantically running into Aimee's bedroom when she was only three after hearing a shriek and hysterical crying. Expecting to find her pinned under a fallen dresser, I instead found her trying to align a seam in her sock, crying, "Oweee! It *hurts.*" Socks—hurt? Sounded farfetched to me at the time, but child-temperament experts explain that we are each born with a certain sensitivity to our environment. Some of us are more sensitive than others to sounds, tastes, smells, and the feel of clothes or human touch. Just being aware of that made me much more patient with Aimee.

Some differences, of course, *are* more complicated. Strong personality traits that are accompanied by motor or speech struggles may indicate a disability. In a later chapter, I'll discuss what parents can do if they suspect their child may have a hidden disability, using the stories of two families whose children do face special challenges.

The book ends with ideas for new attitudes and actions. We can easily go for days without outwardly showing appreciation for our kids. We're either busy dealing with child-related struggles or caught up in our own activities.

You may recall the joke about the wife who says, "You never tell me you love me anymore!" to her hubby. He responds, "I told you so the day we married; when that changes, I'll let you know." We get the joke, because we all know a husband's love should regularly be expressed in his words and actions—just as our love toward our kids should be conveyed.

SOMETIMES WE DO EXPRESS APPRECIATION, BUT NOT IN WAYS THAT REACH OUR CHILD'S HEART.

Sometimes we do express appreciation, but not in ways that reach our child's heart. One thirteen-year-old told me she wished her parents praised her more. I asked how they showed their love to her. She said, "Clothes." This interested me, because kids with expensive clothes are sometimes assumed to be spoiled by their parents.

So I asked, "Would you rather have the clothes or praise?"

"Praise," she replied.

It's important not just to drum up fresh feelings of appreciation, but to express that affirmation in ways most meaningful to your child.

FIRST THINGS FIRST

Before considering what makes your child both incredibly interesting and sometimes hard to live with, you need to look inward. If you struggle with emotional detachment, isolation, or feelings of hopelessness, delighting in your child may seem impossible right now. You are right to be concerned, no matter how "normal" your family appears to outsiders.

Consider what happened one Sunday morning in Ohio in early 2004, when the rear wing of a 114-year-old private school undergoing an expansion project suddenly collapsed, destroying several classrooms and displacing a large number of students.

The accident was unexpected. Outwardly everything had appeared fine. The school had obtained all necessary work permits, and a city inspector had reported no problems following periodic visits. A preliminary assessment concluded that excavation was probably too deep and too close to the existing foundation.[7]

Just as students and staff members noticed nothing unusual the Friday before the building's collapse, a casual friend might assume that all is humming along pretty well in your family. But if you struggle with personal issues that lie close to your foundation—your values, your self-worth, your very soul—you may be surprised one day by an unsettling incident that threatens the stability of your family.

Because delighting in your child is difficult (if not impossible) when you do not understand or value your role as a parent, chapter 2 looks at some common personal struggles that affect parents and offers some ideas on how to address them. Once you identify and attend to them, you'll be free to get to know—and delight in—your one-of-a-kind child.

2

TOUGH STUFF

If God had a refrigerator . . . your picture would be on it.

MAX LUCADO[1]

One day, as I was watching a casual adult baseball game in a local park, a young mother with two wiggly preschoolers sat down nearby. She tried desperately to make her children sit still next to her so she could focus on the game.

To relieve their boredom, the kids began pulling up dandelions from the high weeds growing up beneath their seats, then offered me a droopy bouquet. (You know how dandelions droop the moment you pluck them? Note that in your mind, as I'll reflect back on that later!) I smiled and thought, *What a creative way to kill time.* As they industriously created bouquets for other people nearby, I was startled by a shriek.

"Stop that you two! Put those down! Come here and sit still!"

I thought, *Stop pulling up dandelions? Why?* Apparently the children's activity distracted Mom from watching the players.

But as the game went on, her harsh and critical voice continued relentlessly, making me cringe and distracting everyone else far more than occasional nudges to accept handfuls of flowers from cheery tots.

As I listened to the mom scold her preschoolers that day, I wondered how much she appreciated her children, not just that particular day but in general. Did she estimate and recognize their value, quality, and significance? Was she fully aware of and sensitive to their individuality, as well as the developmental stages they would pass through so quickly? Did she feel thankful to be a mother, and did she enjoy her children?

I CAN APPRECIATE THAT, BUT . . .

The word *appreciate,* usually meaning "enjoy," is sometimes used to mean "understand," as in "I can appreciate that, *but . . .*" It's used to convey the thought, *Although I respect your opinion, I don't agree with you.* In the context of parenting, you may feel that you understand your child pretty well, yet find his behavior difficult to accept. And while correction is often necessary, sometimes too-harsh correction stems from a failure to accept kids for who they are, age-wise and personality-wise.

Perhaps the young mom at the ball game had simply reached the limits of her patience for the day. Yet it saddened me that she did not appear to appreciate—as in, understand—the need for young children to be able to move, at least a little. And worse, she didn't seem to appreciate—as in, enjoy—this precious, tiny window of time during which her preschoolers recognized beauty in simple weeds and so eagerly presented them to strangers.

In my eyes, there was truly nothing wrong with what those children were doing. In fact, they were providing free park maintenance! It was their mother's attitude and actions (including yelling at them) that seemed wrong to me. Yet when I judge her, I feel a stab of guilt. Certainly there have been times when I've responded similarly to my own kids. I've corrected them too quickly or too impatiently, simply because their noise or mess inconvenienced me, or because I was in a cranky mood to begin with.

I too must remember to frequently take deep breaths, stop, and look clearly at what my kids are doing (and why). What in it can I delight in, laugh about? Can I learn to focus on the flowers instead of the outfield?

Yet I know that while choosing to be cheerful is a great idea, it's often not easy. A parent's painful childhood memories, unmet longings or expectations, hidden feelings of guilt, fear, resentment, or sorrow . . . any of those can make it difficult to feel, reveal, and delight fully in the parenting experience.

TOO-HARSH CORRECTION CAN STEM FROM A FAILURE TO ACCEPT KIDS FOR WHO THEY ARE, AGE-WISE AND PERSONALITY-WISE.

Most baby and child-care books devote very few pages to the struggles that parents bring to their role. When dispensing child-care advice, these resources simply can't take into account the individual experiences and situations of their readers.

Likewise, this book provides only a brief overview of several difficult—yet fairly common—attitudes and situations with which you may identify. Yet acknowledging your struggle is the first step in overcoming it. (Be sure to see appendix A for a list of support groups that can help you address these issues further.) Are any of the following stealing your joy in parenting?

LIFESTYLE ISSUES

Frantic Busyness

Have you ever been lost in thought, then startled by a hand waving before your eyes . . . a child impatiently saying, "*He-llo? Anybody home?*" I have. Too often.

When I feel overwhelmed and stressed, I'm not always conscious of a child's presence unless she is literally in my face. And as you can tell, sometimes not even then. I know this frustrates my kids.

Even worse is when I snap at them over minor things. If I catch my son tossing a basketball in the living room when I'm overwhelmed with work, bills, and house responsibilities, my reaction is likely to sound harsh—"I've *told* you a million times *not* to throw the ball in the living room!"—rather than a firm but gentle—"Remember, you need to play ball outside" (while steering him firmly toward the door). My reaction is *absolutely* affected by my stress level. Balls are bigger and bouncier, pictures on walls more breakable, and kids' shrieks louder when I'm stressed.

My reactions are also affected by my self-inflicted schedules. Something is not quite right when I'm asked, "Can I get a ride to Rachel's house?" or "Mom, I need my social security card to apply for that job" and I look absolutely panic-stricken, then blubber endlessly about my lengthy to-do list. My kids look at me as if I'm nuts, asking, "What's the big *deal?*" (which naturally sounds ruder and more demanding when I'm out of sorts).

But what's the big deal, indeed? Do I *really* have to find that rebate slip and mail it? clean the laundry room? drive a child through traffic twice a week to gymnastics classes? How many of those 101 things on my list are truly necessary?

True, it would be nice to get that ten-buck rebate and avoid tripping over the laundry baskets, and I am delighted that Elisa loves gymnastics. But do I have to do all these things, or am I stressing myself out and potentially missing out on the joys of parenting?

At times like this, it helps to divide activities into MUST do, SHOULD do, and CAN do lists. Knock off the "must dos" first, then tackle the "shoulds." Don't forget to ask yourself *why* you feel you should do a certain task: Is it to help reduce the amount of chaos in the home? to help keep the family afloat financially or spiritually? Those are good reasons.

BALLS ARE BIGGER AND BOUNCIER, PICTURES ON WALLS MORE BREAKABLE, AND KIDS' SHRIEKS LOUDER WHEN I'M STRESSED.

Other reasons may not be as good: for instance, feeling you *must* do an activity simply because someone asked and you couldn't say no. Or perhaps you feel you *should* do something—say, bake cookies for a special event or holiday—because, well, that's what good moms do, don't they? In reality store-baked goodies do just fine, with no cleanup time to boot (though of course it's nice to lick the beaters!).

As for "can dos," accept that those may never get done and that's okay. You might move a can-do up the list to a should or even a must, however, if it puts a smile on your hubby's face when he walks in the door or causes your child to impulsively jump on you and give you a smooch. Sometimes the way another person is affected by your efforts is more significant than the task itself.

PHYSICAL ISSUES
Sleep Deprivation
Did you accidentally call your child by your dog's name today or put the remote control in the refrigerator? According to sleep experts, "exhaustion and fatigue affect our emotional moods, causing pessimism, sadness, stress, and anger." Also, "insufficient rest adversely affects the frontal cortex's ability to control speech, access memory, and solve problems." [2]

No wonder prisoners of war are often subjected to sleep deprivation: it depresses them, wears down their defenses, and confuses them! If you are a prisoner of your own schedule, which causes a self-imposed lack of sleep, it's time to give yourself permission to eliminate an activity or two and spend some extra time snoozing. (My mother often took one-hour afternoon naps.)

Most likely, if you have young children or a baby, you are losing sleep involuntarily. But it's not just newborns who keep Mom and Dad awake. As kids grow, they're sometimes needy at night when teething or battling nightmares. Perhaps they are even sleeping well—but you're staying awake worrying about them!

Are you getting enough rest so you can enjoy parenting while you are awake? Is there anything you can do to ensure that your body is getting the sleep it needs? Sleep is so valuable you may occasionally need to call in reinforcements—perhaps help with the kids for an hour so you can crash for a while.

Can you read this without Y A W N I N G?

Medical Problems

For some parents, lack of sleep has little to do with the kids. You may toss and turn all night due to physical discomfort, which turns you into Madam Cranky-Pants the next day. Chronic back pain or a migraine headache may affect you any time of day, distracting you from delighting in your kids when you're trying to cope with extreme discomfort or side effects from medicines.

Some medical problems are complicated when parents forget to protect their own physical health during the manual labor aspects of parenting. Hauling a kicking and screaming thirty-pound toddler-turning-preschooler the entire length of a mall will make your back cry out later. Inadequate nutrition due to being "too busy" to eat properly can affect blood sugar levels—and moods toward kids. Try not to trade away your wellness exams, physical therapy appointments, or other needed appointments for kid-related activities.

Even something as simple as chronic allergies can interfere with joy and energy for fun parenting. For years I felt as if I had the worst head cold imaginable—all day every day in spring— unless I took medication, which then made me too sleepy to play with my kids. Hormonal cycles and hormone-related treatments can cause emotions to run high and even become explosive when imbalanced.

Pay attention to what your body is doing. Do physical changes or pain affect your emotional reactions toward your kids? If so, be honest with your doctor about that.

Depression, including postpartum depression, is a medical issue for which treatment is available. New moms are especially vulnerable to feelings of depression; about 10 percent of new moms experience postpartum depression in the first year following their baby's birth.[3] (A very small percentage experience postpartum psychosis.) Feelings of sadness, anxiety, and hopelessness; fatigue; and a loss of interest in hobbies, eating, and other pleasurable activities may be signs of postpartum depression.

It is imperative that moms with this condition talk with their doctors, accept help from others, and set realistic goals for themselves. It's also important that they set aside time for exercise and other enjoyable activities. Of course, this counsel applies to any mom or dad who feels overwhelmed by parenting.

EMOTIONAL ISSUES
Ambivalence about Parenthood
Perhaps it's a dirty little secret, but at some point most parents feel ambivalent about their parenting responsibilities. Often it first hits shortly after Mom and Dad bring home a squawling baby to a house that suddenly seems to be in a constant state of upheaval. On days when the words *work clothes* mean spit-up stained shoulders or when you long to jump in the car and go without buckling a car seat (but can't even find ten minutes to shower and make yourself presentable), parenthood may truly feel like a sacrifice.

If you struggle with feelings of ambivalence, don't be afraid to admit your struggles—to God and to others—but don't overlook the delights that parenting can bring. When your baby's dimply fingers catch in your hair and he pulls your face to his in one of those funny wide-open-mouthed kisses, or when your five-year-old gives you a drawing of "Mommy and Me" with giant hearts around it, savor each moment.

Have you ever been impatiently herding your child through the checkout at a grocery store or a mall department store, only to be stopped by an elderly woman who tells you, "Enjoy your children while they're young—the time goes by so fast"? That wise senior is simply verbalizing the "sequencing concept": Parenthood is demanding for about eighteen years; after that comes a lot of free time to fit in everything else.

PERHAPS IT'S A DIRTY LITTLE SECRET, BUT AT SOME POINT MOST PARENTS FEEL AMBIVALENT ABOUT THEIR RESPONSIBILITY.

When you're in the thick of parenting, sometimes it helps to talk with other moms who also struggle in mothering. (See appendix A for a list of resources.)

Isolation

One mom told me that when her son was about two, she wanted to run away from home. She'd moved to a new town and felt she could not ask anyone to give her a break from caring for her demanding young son. Her husband didn't understand the effect that isolation was having on her when he was working overtime, nor did he understand her need to get out of the house for a break when he was home.

One day she'd reached her limit. The moment he walked in

the door, she said she was going out. He asked, "Where to?" and she replied, "Anywhere!" After driving around for a while, she returned calmer and better able to help her husband understand her need for some time alone.

Some of this mom's difficulties came because she had a strong-willed child, but her isolation made her more vulnerable to anxiety and depression. The good news is that now, six years later, she ministers to other struggling moms.

If you are a single parent, the need for outside friendship and support is even more critical. You need hands-on help and periodic breaks. But you also need—as much as or more than anyone else—to reserve small bits of time to focus on your kids. This will enhance your delight in them and bolster their confidence in your love.

It may take courage on your part to look for and approach other parents, but we all need companionship and support from others dealing with issues similar to ours. However, if you long for a close friendship, I also urge you to begin asking God to send you a friend who will support you emotionally and spiritually, who will stick "closer than a brother" (Proverbs 18:24). When at age twenty I earnestly prayed that prayer, God sent me Cyndi, who had prayed that same prayer and who has been like a sister to me for twenty-seven years.

Although Cyndi has never been able to have children of her own, she adores mine and shows amazing discernment regarding their personalities and needs. Even more valuable is that she knows me, has faith in me, and trusts my judgment. When I clash with my kids, Cyndi and Gordy help me

COPING WITH PARENTING STRUGGLES

1. Acknowledge that one (or more) of the areas discussed in this chapter is an issue for you, and realize you are not alone.

2. Depending on the issue, seek support from a professional or from other parents who also struggle in this area.

3. Don't underestimate the value of prayer and turning concerns over to God.

Lord, you know I'm struggling right now. I really need your help so I can experience less anxiety [or exhaustion, or pain, or anger, or loneliness] and enjoy being a parent more. Please direct me to people who can help me, and give me your comfort and healing. Help me to treasure my children.

keep my perspective, reminding me of what I do right and of my kids' positive attributes. Sometimes I wonder if I would have missed out on this heaven-sent friendship had I not asked for it.

If you need a friend, have you asked God for one? Meanwhile, pray that *you* will learn to be the kind of friend someone else needs.

Marital or Other Stresses

Nothing can interfere more with the parent-child relationship than the parent-parent relationship. When emotions are in an uproar because of hurts within a marriage, the kids will feel that tension and may even get sucked into parental battles.

And, of course, in those circumstances it's easy for an angry parent to overlook his or her kid's positive attributes. If you see this happening, I urge you to work hard with your spouse to address your issues or to get outside help so that you have energy to focus on your kids.

By the same token, if you are playful and joyful with your spouse, that will overflow into delight with your kids. When I say in front of my kids, "Your dad is *such* a hunk!" and the two of us kiss, the children say "Eeuuw!" But often we all end up in a group hug or family tickle-fest.

Other worries—for instance, financial concerns (Does that envelope have another bill stamped "PAST DUE" in it?) or problems related to work (How will I ever meet that deadline?) or extended family (Will Grandma make it through that hip operation?)—will affect the way we interact with our kids unless we deliberately choose not to let them.

Unfortunately, it's too easy to spend all day thinking about a problem and not really notice our kids. We have to find a way to deal with issues and then deliberately put them aside to enjoy our children.

ISSUES FROM THE PAST THAT INVADE THE PRESENT

If you are dissatisfied with your interactions with your kids and chronically fight negative feelings about life in general, you are likely being influenced by deeper, perhaps unresolved, issues. Since in this particular book my focus is on what makes your kids remarkable and delightful, the following descriptions of deeper issues are brief. However, appendix A lists resources that may be helpful if you decide that these concerns significantly prevent you from rejoicing in parenting.

Emotional Abuse and Anger

If you experienced neglect or emotional abuse as a child, you are likely to struggle with finding joy in parenting, especially if you have unresolved anger or a low self-image as a result of the abuse. However, it takes some exploration and a lot of insight to realize exactly how your reactions to your kids are connected with your past.

In her book on motherhood anger, *She's Gonna Blow,* Julie Ann Barnhill mentions how parents who were abused as children may struggle to control anger with their own kids. They may also have difficulty bonding with their children. If you didn't experience healthy appreciation as a child, it may be hard for you to express that to your own kids. If you were never told "I love you," it may feel strange saying that to your child.

WHEN YOUR CHILD BECOMES SASSY OR OUT OF CONTROL, UNHEALTHY SCRIPTS FROM YOUR CHILDHOOD MAY COME UNBIDDEN TO MIND.

Yet if you are dedicated to parenting—as I suspect you are, since you're reading this book—it's possible that you praise your child in ways you never were praised, saying things like, "You're a great kid, you know?" Meanwhile you may feel an underlying sadness that you weren't told that yourself, and despite praising your child, you may not feel true delight in her. Are you a good parent, but not necessarily a happy one?

When your child becomes sassy or out of control, do unhealthy scripts from your childhood come unbidden to mind?

Even parents from healthy families can find it hard to come up with perfectly mature, adult, caring, clear responses when kids are angry and say, "You *always*..." or "You *never*...!" or perhaps even "I *hate* you!" It can be hard to be the grown-up when your own feelings are hurt and to know how to express feelings in positive ways instead of crying or denying those emotions.

In a touching yet funny moment, five-year-old Imani (Cameron's sister) was terribly upset with Elisa, who—usually rich in sensitivity—was that day impatient and intolerant (as we all can be). When Elisa abruptly decided she'd spent enough time playing and said so while walking away, Imani burst into tears.

Imani then so aptly described the range of emotions she was feeling. She sank down on our stairs, sobbing, "E—E—Elisa, she's just pushin' *all* my buttons ... [hiccup, wail] ... the green ones, and the yellow ones, the *red* ones ..."

Although I'm unsure which colors represented which emotions—jealousy, bewilderment, and anger were apparent—I loved this expression of her feelings and her ability to show that kids certainly do know how to push not only each other's buttons but ours too. My son is an expert at pushing mine—often deliberately—and I find myself responding to him in the same way my own parents reacted when I acted out as a teen. I'm thankful that they never responded with insults or put-downs, even when emotions were running high. Though your parents may have put you down, if you stick with the issues at hand and never insult your child's character, you've taken the first best step toward delighting in and appreciating your child.

Self-Criticism

Jesus said the second greatest commandment is to "Love your neighbor as yourself" (Matthew 22:39). Behind that is the assumption that you cannot accept and give love to others until you appreciate yourself.

It's certainly hard to feel loving toward other people if you feel crummy about yourself, isn't it? If you have a tendency to put yourself down, especially because of a lack of nurturing in your own childhood, it may be wise to explore with a counselor or mentor exactly what compels you to do that. If you don't change that tendency, your kids are likely to pick up on it and become self-critical too.

Most important is that you recognize God's love and delight for you personally. As you read the next chapter describing the amazing complexity of the human body and spirit, remember that *you* were once a baby lovingly crafted by God in your own mother's womb, and God destined for you to parent the child you have today. He rejoices in you. Can you believe that?

It's hard for a downcast parent to uplift a child. The saying "When Mama ain't happy, ain't nobody happy" certainly has merit, doesn't it? That goes for dads, too.

You owe it to your child and yourself to explore what makes *you* feel valuable and loved. Fortunately, God Himself wants to help you. "Into our weary world, our shattered dreams and broken hearts, God sent a . . . healer in disguise. You would need to be desperate to find Him, but to those who are desperate, He is here!" says Christian singer, speaker, and author Sheila Walsh, who herself battled depression for many years.[4]

Grief

Nearly every year during the week of my father's birth, as well as the week of his death from a traffic accident, I feel a deep sadness, even when I'm not consciously aware of the date. Eventually one of my kids will ask, "What's wrong, Mom?" and I realize that my body clock followed the calendar even if my mind didn't.

The loss of a loved one, including a child by miscarriage, sudden infant death syndrome, or illness or injury later in life, can cause subconscious grieving on recurring dates. Even many years later the hurt can still be there, although some might callously ask, "It's been so long. . . . Aren't you over that yet?"

Also, anyone who has had an abortion may feel emotional pain on dates related to that, and it's possible that unresolved feelings of guilt or sadness may affect a mother's delight in life and her living children. Many of these women, especially within churches, suffer in silence, not realizing that support and understanding are available. Thankfully a number of ministries reach out to postabortive women,[5] and Scripture offers promises of comfort and reassurance of forgiveness.

If you've lost a child, no matter what the cause, you're likely to feel an aching sense of loss for a missing person in your family constellation. Even as I wrote the following chapter, which explores the amazing intricacy of the preborn child, I was surprised to find myself thinking about a baby I miscarried and wondering what kind of personality that child would have had—or has now in heaven.

As for coping with the loss of my dad, I've found that it's healthier to deliberately process that grief—for instance, to look at pictures of him on his birthday and talk about his personality with my kids—rather than try to distract myself with busyness and be unexplainably snappy or distant. (Of course, some losses you may need to process with other adults rather than burdening your children with them.)

It's also healing to consciously and deliberately delight in kids on days we suspect will be difficult. Focus on your children's marvelous attributes. Accept nurture in their hugs and kisses. Thank God for them!

TAKE ME BACK TO THE BALL GAME

Remember my comment about how that young mother needed to focus more on the flowers instead of the outfield? Well, it may be that in her infield she was dealing with any number of the issues mentioned in this chapter. She may have been stressed and exhausted, ambivalent about motherhood, lonely, angry, self-critical, or even grieving.

But the end result was that she could not see what was immediately before her: how her precious children were quickly growing "like weeds" and how her harsh comments, if too frequent, would eventually cause her children to droop as dandelions do only a few hours after picking.

The same week I wrote down the opening story about the woman at the ball field, I was startled by a conversation Elisa and I had as I walked her to school.

"I'm so excited I got a solo!" she said, referring to an upcoming first-grade music performance. But she added that she was sad that one of her best friends hadn't gotten a solo part too.

"She felt so bad, Mom, she really drooped. Like this . . ." Elisa slumped her shoulders and put on a downcast face.

I was amazed that Elisa had chosen the word *drooped*—the same one I'd chosen to represent a child's reaction to disappointment and feelings of rejection.

Not every child, of course, can sing a solo in the first-grade musical. But *every* child should have the opportunity to shine brightly within his or her own home, like a sunny yellow dandelion. Your love for your child will nurture him just as warm sun and quenching rain makes that little flower bloom. Just as a dandelion grows sturdily despite exposure to harsh weather or careless trampling from feet under park bleachers, a child who is accepted and encouraged will be more able to weather terrible, horrible, no good, very bad days.

EVERY CHILD SHOULD HAVE THE OPPORTUNITY TO SHINE BRIGHTLY WITHIN HIS OR HER OWN HOME.

If you yourself need light and watering, I suggest you utilize some of the tips and resources I offer within these pages. I also invite you to look to the Light of the World and the Living Water—Jesus—who extends to you His love and acceptance and encouragement. If you have difficulty allowing His grace to seep into your spirit, I encourage you to immerse yourself in His Word. One easy way to do this, especially whenever you feel anxious, fearful, or depressed, is to soak up a few of God's promises. (Try *The Bible Promise Book* or *Touchpoints Bible Promises.*[6]) My favorite promise comes from Philippians 4:6-7, where Paul reminds us to not be anxious, and tells us that with earnest prayer we'll be given a peace that is beyond human understanding.

Now let's move on to a story about a little animated ant named Flik, which I hope will make you aware not just of your child's potential and value but of your own!

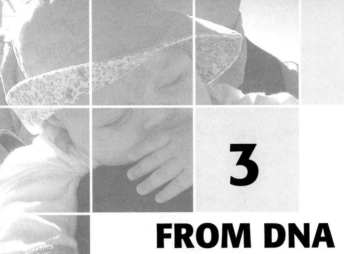

3

FROM DNA TO BIRTH DAY

*The being that is now you or I
is the same being that was once an adolescent,
and before that a toddler,
and before that an infant,
and before that a fetus,
and before that an embryo.
To have destroyed the being that is you or me at any of these stages
would have been to destroy you or me.*

ROBERT P. GEORGE
PRINCETON UNIVERSITY'S MCCORMICK PROFESSOR OF JURISPRUDENCE
AND MEMBER OF THE PRESIDENT'S COUNCIL ON BIOETHICS[1]

In the animated film *A Bug's Life,* Flik the ant attempts to reassure little ant Dot about his abilities and significance when Dot complains that he feels useless.

"See that tree?" says Flik. "Everything that made that *giant* tree is already contained in this little seed." He elaborates, then continues, "All it needs is some time, a little bit of sunshine, and some rain, and voilà! . . ."[2]

Flik reassures Dot that, like the seed, he has enormous potential. I think it is significant that later in the film, when Flik is feeling worthless because he has goofed (as he repeatedly does), he is reminded by Dot that he too started off like a seed, full of potential. Spurred on, Flik uses his creativity and determination to save his entire ant community. Likewise, much that makes your child unique—and praiseworthy—was developed long before birth, even when he was no larger than a seed.

WHERE DID *THAT* COME FROM?

Even before I was pregnant with Tyler, he was destined to have blue eyes like his grandma Jill. And since the time Aimee was a baby, I've occasionally glimpsed in her face an expression my grandma Gladys used to make. It catches me off guard and makes me catch my breath. Your child may also have mannerisms that uncannily remind you of yourself or someone else in your family.

The recipe for your child's nature—his or her DNA—was decided upon long before you loosened the waist of your jeans, then upgraded to maternity garb. Before your child was born, it was determined whether her hair would be black and curly or blonde and straight, whether her skin would be reminiscent of porcelain or warm cocoa. It was dictated how her nose would turn up or down, how her eyebrows would arch, and perhaps even that she might be a relentless foot tapper.

Within the little seed from which your child sprouted was a combination of her physical attributes, abilities, and preferences that already made her different from any other child: a unique blend of inherited genetic traits.

At only nine weeks after conception, her fingerprints began to form: prints that the FBI could still use to distinguish her from anyone else, including relatives, when she is ninety. Even identical twins, who share the same DNA, have subtle differences in their fingerprints. (As the child grows in her mom's womb, her developing fingers reach out and press against her surroundings, affecting the height of the fingerprint ridges, although the predetermined pattern of the swirls remains.)[3]

Fingerprinting used to be the primary method for identification, but due to recent developments in forensic science, suspects can now be convicted based on DNA found in a strand of hair. Security doors can be opened to employees through retina recognition.

How can your retina be so different from mine or anyone else's? What causes one human cell to become part of the retina rather than a muscle cell? How does each cell know what to do?

While leaving that last question unanswered, author Barry Werth captures the marvel of this process well in the book *From Conception to Birth: A Life Unfolds.* The book contains spectacular photos by Alexander Tsiaras, using state-of-the-art imaging technologies to reveal embryonic and fetal development.

In the accompanying text—referring to the miraculous cell division that begins at conception—Werth writes: "Imagine yourself as the world's tallest skyscraper, built in nine months and germinating from a single brick." He invites the reader to picture that single brick dividing into every other type of material needed to manufacture that enormous building and its contents: tons of steel, glass, and concrete; miles of cable and electrical wiring; furniture; computer systems; and much more. And what if that building had the "capacity to love, hate, do calculus, compose symphonies"?[4] It sounds ridiculous, doesn't it? Yet such a scenario is not all that different from the indescribable development of a baby in the womb. How amazingly complex we are!

Many people believe that all this somehow happens spontaneously, with no grand architect or builder. Others with a deep understanding of anatomy and physiology do see a grand architect behind it all.

The late Dr. Paul Wilson Brand, who had been clinical professor emeritus in orthopedics at the University of Washington, was a brilliant pioneer in the research of Hansen's Disease (leprosy). He performed thousands of surgeries and authored a clinical manual of hand mechanics for surgeons and therapists.

Brand revealed his understanding of God as designer in his book *Fearfully and Wonderfully Made,* coauthored with Philip Yancey. He compared people within the body of Christ (the church) to cells within the human body in an intriguing way, but he also included details about the complexity of the human body from a biological standpoint.

He posed the hypothetical question: "What ushers in the higher specialized functions of movement, sight, and consciousness through the coordination of a hundred trillion cells?" He noted that a nerve cell alone "branches out and unites the body with a computer network of dazzling sophistication." (Brand studied nerve cells intently, because leprosy deformities are caused by the lack of proper nerve cell function—sensation—allowing frequent, permanent injury to limbs. In other words, pain is our friend.)

Brand then described the complexity of DNA *within* each cell: one hundred thousand genes containing instructions that "if written out, would fill a thousand six-hundred-page books."[5]

AWE OR EXPLOITATION?

Modern advances in reproductive technology and genetic engineering certainly affirm the wonders of the human body and the human embryo. And since science now confirms that each embryo contains its own genetic blueprint—as do the egg and sperm that joined to form it—new ethical quagmires emerge. We are offered fresh opportunities for exploitation as well as awe.

Some parents—hopefully a rare few—see these advances as opportunities to *choose* genetic characteristics they want in their kids. In the article "Designer Babies," author and lawyer Lori B. Andrews writes about several bizarre court cases related to child choosing.

In one case, *Harnicher v. University of Utah Medical Center,* a couple sued because when their triplets were born—as a result of in vitro fertilization—one child had red hair instead of brown. Apparently in the lab, sperm donor #183 had been confused with #83. The couple claimed that the "disappointment" in their children—preferring the looks of the other do-nor—caused them "severe emotional distress to the point of mental illness." [6]

The couple lost the case, although some lawmakers felt it had merit (after all, the couple didn't receive the product they'd paid for, right?). I can only pray that those parents now treasure their three precious children, who by now must be funny and affectionate preschoolers. Despite their technological beginnings, despite their hair color, each of those children is a unique human being with the power to contribute immeasurably to their parents' life and the life of others.

ONE-OF-A-KIND WONDER

I'm actually quite relieved that I didn't have to choose my own kids' characteristics. Good grief, I can't even decide what color to paint the living room. Friends who have built homes from scratch—forced to make hundreds of small decisions about every gadget in the kitchen and bath—tell me that in hindsight, living with some of those decisions is different from what they imagined. I guess you just don't know what it's like to use the toaster until you've moved in, then try to plug it into an outlet that's in the wrong place.

In my wildest dreams, I could never have imagined the intriguing variety of attributes my own children would have, let alone have chosen between those possible features. After all, I would have no idea what it would be like to actually *live* with a child with those traits. Would I have chosen stubbornness as a desired attribute? Not likely. But living with stubborn kids has helped me appreciate and respect their positive persistence and determination. And my being forced to deal with less-than-compliant people has grown my own character as well.

I'm grateful that my only decision with each pregnancy was simply to *choose* the child I'd been given and to accept each one as a gift. In fact, by the time my third child was born, I couldn't wait to meet her. I knew she'd be a one-of-a-kind creation, just as my first two had been—full of surprises.

A person's individuality goes much deeper even than what is ordained by his or her genetic code, as Larry Burkett and Rick Osborne point out in their book, *Your Child Wonderfully Made.* The inner person—one's thoughts, feelings, moral sensitivity—is a gift from God as well. Your child's spirit, matched by God with his genetic makeup, further distinguishes him from everyone else.[7]

I'M GRATEFUL THAT MY ONLY DECISION WITH EACH PREGNANCY WAS SIMPLY TO *CHOOSE* THE CHILD I'D BEEN GIVEN AND ACCEPT EACH ONE AS A GIFT.

In the old novel *The Stepford Wives* (which has spawned two movie adaptations), the main character moves to a small town and is disturbed by the way all the women in town act alike. She discovers with horror that all the husbands in town, seeking "perfect" wives, have replaced their flesh-and-bone women with robots that have retained their wives' individual looks yet have been given identical personalities.

Do we really want an army of bland Stepford children in a quest for that "perfect" child? Or are we willing to accept the potluck of personalities that God offers us?

THE NURTURE BEGINS: IN THE WOMB

Your child's *nature,* his genetic traits coupled with his spirit, begins to be affected by *nurture* even before birth. One fascinating article in *Psychology Today* describes what a fetus most likely hears, sees, feels, and tastes when in the womb.

Take hearing, for example. Since newborns usually hear perfectly well at birth, researchers wondered, *What exactly do they hear within the womb?*

A hydrophone placed inside the uterus of a pregnant woman revealed that, besides the rush of fluids and her heartbeat, the fetus can hear noises outside of the womb. The sound level is compared to what we might overhear in an upstairs apartment: yelling, slamming doors, loud music, and voices.[8]

In another study, newborns were tested to see if they could recognize their mother's voice as well as the rhythm of *The Cat in The Hat,* which had been read aloud to them while they were still in the womb. Sure enough, accelerated sucking patterns revealed preferences for the familiar, from Mom's voice to the cadence of Dr. Seuss rhymes.

I find it exciting to know that my children were uniquely designed from the start, but also to realize that before I even held them in my arms for the first time they likely knew my voice!

WHEN THINGS GO WRONG

Sadly, sometimes things go awry in the womb or cause trauma as a child exits from it. Such a setback can prevent a child from reaching the capabilities his genetic blueprint would otherwise have dictated.

Sometimes babies are simply born too early and their tiny bodies are not yet ready to face the world. Sometimes heroic efforts are required to save them, though in this new century, the age of viability is becoming younger and younger, as described in the fascinating book *Before Their Time: Lessons in Living from Those Born Too Soon.* This book profiles five families whose babies were born at between twenty-four and twenty-eight weeks gestation. (Many premature infants, even ones born this early, not only live but go on to lead normal lives.) Even those babies who struggled or lost their lives displayed unique features and personalities. One baby boy in particular, whom the nurses did not expect to live, not only survived but amazed the medical staff with his tenacity.[9]

It's critical to realize that every child born with physical or mental impairments is a unique person.

Rosalie Icenhower describes the joy her developmentally delayed daughter, Becky, brings her family in Rosalie's book *Don't Sing Any Sad Songs: A Down Syndrome Daughter's Joyful Journey.*[10] Becky lives in a group home, has a job, and has traveled to Europe.

Individuals with disabilities sometimes impact the world in ways most fully abled people never will. Bill Porter, a man born with cerebral palsy, has a severe speech impediment and multiple other physical struggles. The exact cause of Bill's handicaps are unknown, but cerebral palsy can be caused by a lack of oxygen to the brain during pregnancy or delivery (sometimes caused by use of forceps) or other unknown factors.

Bill's mother was told at his birth to institutionalize him—

apparently a too-common suggestion in the 1940s. She chose instead to devote her life to her child.

The combination of Bill's innate personality and his mother's support led him—despite his physical limitations—to grow up to become a top Watkins products salesman and the inspiration behind the movie *Door to Door*.[11] Bill's mother gave him the courage to use his inborn talents and personality traits in ways that helped him succeed, even while dealing with an uncooperative body.

But even more important than his achievement of personal success is the impact Bill has had on thousands of other people's lives, especially after the movie about his life was televised. Many perfectly able-bodied individuals have written him to thank him for the courage he's given them.

For many years Bill, who is unable to drive, got up every morning at 4:30. That gave him time to dress impeccably, take a bus to his assigned district, then trudge (even in nasty weather) for more than eight hours a day to achieve his personal sales goals. Even when eight out of ten doors were shut in his face, he remained optimistic, ever hopeful that "the next person will say yes." He doggedly returned to those who initially had said no until many became dedicated, lifelong customers.

Bill's unique determination and optimism helped him pursue a job he was gifted at and loved. Don't we want that for our kids as well? Many people born with all body parts in complete working order never find a job they eagerly jump out of bed at 4:30 a.m. to do!

Another inspiration to me is a fourteen-year-old young man named Gabe Murfitt, whose disability is reminiscent of many of those babies whose mothers took the drug thalidomide to combat morning sickness in the late 1950s and early 1960s.

Two of the major bones in Gabe's legs are fused together so that he cannot uncross them. His arms are only two inches long, so his hands are where elbows should be. Yet his personality shines so brightly that he caught the attention of television producers for *Good Morning America* and *The Oprah Winfrey Show*. Why? For starters, he was seen climbing out of his wheelchair to join his junior high basketball team on the court. He did the same at a junior high dance: he rocked on the floor as his date danced on her knees with him.

The show producers marveled at Gabe's self-confidence and determination. But they did not seem to inquire deeply enough about what I think is most critical: What makes Gabe that way? How do family and faith impact who Gabe is?

In a later chapter I'll introduce you to the Murfitt family and reveal how their appreciation of personality differences, coupled with their faith in God, is triumphing over adversity that comes with disability.

WHAT'S SO SPECIAL ABOUT *YOUR* CHILD?

Bill and Gabe have different life stories and have impacted people in different ways. What makes their stories similar is that they were both born with a severe disability to parents who refused to allow that diagnosis to prevent their son from accomplishing all that he could.

As it turns out, Bill's and Gabe's physical struggles are being used by God as a way to showcase their personalities. There's a mystery there that the movie and television show producers sensed: How can a person facing so many physical challenges have such self-confidence and determination? Yet to me it's less a mystery than a rich lesson to embrace; the example set by their families can encourage us to instill similar optimism in our own children.

DO YOU MARVEL AT YOUR CHILDREN'S COMPLEX DESIGN AND RECOGNIZE THE PRIVILEGE YOU HAVE TO HELP THEM REACH THEIR POTENTIAL?

You see, the reality is that many bright, athletic, young people never reach their potential, due to lack of encouragement from a mother or father. Gabe Murfitt's lot in life is far better than that of a child or teen who goes through life never hearing "How was your day?" "Don't stay out too late or I'll worry," or more important, "You're a terrific kid. I love you!" Some children grow into adulthood never being told of their value and significance.

I believe you love and want the best for your child. But do you truly embrace her on a day-to-day basis? Do you marvel at her complex design and recognize the privilege you have to care for her and help her reach her potential?

UNWRAPPING THE GIFT

On my wedding day years ago, I received a beautiful crystal vase. Since then, I've kept it in my china cabinet and reserved it for special occasions, like holding a birthday rose.

Recently I realized that I've probably spent more time and energy over the years protecting it or cleaning it than I have enjoying it. "Kids!" I've cried out many times, "no cartwheels by the china cabinet! Something will get broken."

I've forgotten who gave me that vase and have no idea how it was created. It wasn't until recently that I actually stopped to examine it closely. I was amazed to see patterns in the cut glass that I had never noticed in twenty-five years!

Your child was designed in a complex and marvelous way from the start. The closer you look at him and listen to him, the more unique details you will see. Yet unlike a factory-made crystal vase, your child is a one-of-a-kind creation.

To get a better sense of your child's uniqueness and significance from the moment of conception, you might try personalizing Psalm 139:13-16. You might even retype it, inserting your child's name, and then post it on your refrigerator:

> For you created [my child's] inmost being; you knit [him/her] together in my . . . womb. I praise you because [my child is] fearfully and wonderfully made; your works are wonderful, I know that full well. [My child's] frame was not hidden from you when [he/she] was made in the secret place. When [he/she] was woven together in the depths of the earth, your eyes saw [his/her] unformed body. All the days ordained for [my child] were written in your book before one of them came to be.

In the next chapter, you will be challenged to find new and creative ways to get to know your child's personality. How can you become or remain sensitive to the differences between you and your child? How do personality differences impact and enrich you and your family?

4

PERSONALITY POTLUCK

*When the time came for [Rebekah] to give birth,
there were twin boys in her womb. . . . The boys grew up,
and Esau became a skillful hunter, a man of the open country,
while Jacob was a quiet man, staying among the tents.*

GENESIS 25:24, 27

Long before Elisa and Aimee jumped and wiggled their way into this world, I became fascinated with personality traits in children.

It all started when my first child, Tyler, was old enough to clearly let me know what was on his mind. Being a bright kid and an early talker, he challenged me sooner than expected. I quickly realized I'd delivered not just a child, but a challenge!

My son was a pint-sized lawyer, constantly negotiating, for instance, the number of cookies he could have without spoiling his appetite for dinner an hour later.

"One," I'd say.

"Three!" he'd say with a grin before reassuring me that of *course* he'd be a faithful member of the clean-plate club.

"Two," I'd say, sighing. Then would come the next round of cheerful (okay, sometimes not-so-cheerful) negotiations surrounding teeth brushing or bedtime.

Frequent cries of "Me do myself!" at age two and sometimes "You're not the boss of me!" at age three continually reminded me that this child was fiercely determined. All toddlers can be stubborn, of course. Yet my son seemed to have an exceptionally strong willful streak. He was also charmingly affectionate and funny, comically exaggerating the expressions of people in magazine pictures just to make us laugh.

I remember wondering, *How much of his behavior is developmentally related? Are all toddlers this stubborn? this cuddly? this observant and funny? Or is his personality unique?*

Tyler's thought processes alternately thrilled, disconcerted, and maddened me.

As a young preschooler, he said he wanted to learn about cars. At the library I found him a picture book of model cars.

"No!" he cried out impatiently, casting the book down. "I want to know why the car goes when you push that thing with your foot!"

Oh! I recall thinking. *He wants to know how engines work? Wow.*

It was thrilling to realize how his mind was working, yet disconcerting to realize that he was already asking questions for which I didn't have immediate answers. The maddening part came as he also began questioning—then learning—the rules of the road, such as why signals should be used before turning or when headlights should be dimmed on dark roads.

"Mom, you forgot your clicker," he'd remind me gleefully.

"Cut your brights!" he'd quickly instruct me, before I had a chance to keep from blinding an oncoming car.

Cute, but not really. The only thing worse than a backseat driver is one sitting in a booster seat who hasn't even outgrown night diapers yet!

But sometimes the insights that came from the booster seat were profound. One evening as we drove home after viewing an Easter passion play, Tyler was quiet for a long time.

He then said softly, "Jesus didn't have to die on that cross. He coulda gotten down off it, but He didn't. He did it to save us."

WE AREN'T DESTINED MERELY TO RAISE OUR CHILDREN BUT TO SPEND A LIFETIME GETTING TO KNOW THEM.

The same bright child who'd been determined to find out how engines work was thinking deeply about how God works. Yes, I'd shared the gospel with him in the past. But Tyler's insightful conclusion that Jesus could have gotten down from the cross was his own. It brought tears to my eyes. And it reminded me that our children are not merely genetically orchestrated personalities—they are spiritual creatures too.

Tyler now drives his own battered 1986 pickup, caring less about *how* it runs than *if* it runs! As he's grown, I've been reminded constantly that his personality differs greatly from mine, from his dad's, from his sisters'. I've never met another person like him. I never expect to.

I've realized that I wasn't destined to merely raise my son but to spend a lifetime getting to know him.

TEMPERAMENT ABCS

A animated • adventurous • analytical • adaptable • artistic • affectionate • anxious

B bouncy • bold • balanced • blunt • brazen

C caring • cautious • cheerful • competitive • confident • considerate • consistent • convincing • contemplative • courageous • creative

D demonstrative • dramatic • daring • decisive • detailed • deep • diplomatic • determined • dreamer

E effervescent • efficient • emotional • energetic • entertaining • enthusiastic • ethical • extroverted

F faithful • fearful • frank • funny • friendly • forgiving

G gallant • gleeful • gracious • grateful • gregarious • go-getter

H honest • hotheaded • hospitable • humble • humorous

I innocent • inspiring • independent • idealistic • introverted

J jaunty • joiner • jolly • joyful • just

K kind • killjoy • knowing

L leader • lively • logical • loyal • listener

M merry • musical • mediator • moody • meditative

N naive • negotiator • noisy • no-nonsense • nonconforming • nurturing

O objective • optimistic • orderly • outspoken • obliging

P playful • positive • persuasive • productive • persistent • prankster • peaceful • patient • pleasant • pessimistic

Q quick-tempered • quick-witted • quiet • quality-oriented • questioning

R resourceful • respectful • reserved • refreshing • reverent • rhythmic

S sassy • sociable • serious • spirited • spontaneous • self-reliant • self-sacrificing • sensitive • scheduled • self-controlled • shy • spiritual • stubborn

T take-charge • talkative • tenacious • tender • thoughtful • tolerant • thrill seeker • tough

U unbending • unconventional • understanding • unemotional • uninhibited • uplifting

V vain • verbal • vocal • vigilant • virtuous • vivacious

W wiggly • winsome • wise • wistful • witty

X Xacting (okay, I cheated on that one) • Does Xuberant count?

Y yearning • yielding

Z zany • zealous • zestful

ALLOW ME TO INTRODUCE . . . !

How well do you know your own child? Are you excited about the chance to get to know your son or daughter as a unique human being—someone you will only *begin* to appreciate in the few years he or she lives under your roof?

Your child no doubt possesses a combination of traits that surprise and intrigue you. To begin thinking about what character traits are most predominant in your child, take a look at the "Temperament ABCs" chart on pages 54–55. Don't spend a lot of time trying to analyze each word. This is not a personality test, just a simple activity to help you begin thinking about how your child typically responds to his surroundings.

As you read the list, what words jumped out at you immediately, describing what you see most strongly and frequently in your son or daughter? Which traits do you recall seeing in your child since he or she first began to walk and talk—maybe even before that?

Your child's strongest traits are often those you find yourself trying to tone down—especially if those traits are opposite from the ones you were born with. For example, if your child is superenergetic and you are more calm and quiet, you may say "Settle down, please!" a dozen times a day.

On the flip side, you may try to cultivate those traits that come *less* naturally to your child. If you are extroverted and have a shy child, you may urge him impatiently to let go of your pant leg and join the throng of other children. And while he may remain naturally shy, he eventually is likely to learn that joining other kids—even when he feels uncomfortable—can lead to making new friends.

For this reason, a child may express opposite traits, depending on time and place, expectations and experience. He may be bold and adventurous at times, yet exercise caution and good judgment when needed. But what characterizes your child most strongly? Would you say he is *mostly* adventurous or *mostly* cautious?

An adventurous toddler will jump pell-mell into a pool of busy children, while a more cautious one tends to hang back—testing the water before tentatively dipping in. An older cautious child may jump on a trampoline, yet be relieved that it has a net to keep him from falling out. His adventurous and impulsive friend, however, may deliberately try to bounce out, up, and over the nine-foot barrier. If successful, he may bump his head on the picnic table, laugh, then do it all over again!

Adventurous kids cause parents' hair to go gray early. But more timid children can worry parents as well, as they often need an extra push in life to make the most of their other attributes.

How a child uses his inborn traits—whether those will be strengthened or subdued—will be influenced throughout his childhood by three or four factors:

1. **Relationships.** Your relationship with your child will have a greater impact on him than that of any other person, so do all you can to nurture him. Also seek to help him develop mutually uplifting relationships with siblings, grandparents, friends, and others.
2. **The way he is educated.** Be involved in your child's education to ensure that your child's classroom is suited to

his makeup. I'm not suggesting that you ask his teacher to cater to your child but to be sure she recognizes his personality traits, builds up his strengths, and encourages him to overcome weaknesses. In some cases, you may even decide that homeschooling is the best option for you and your child.

3. **The environment in which he lives.** Make sure your household provides your child a rich environment—and I'm not talking about material trappings. Two children with similar personalities—one of whom isn't appreciated and encouraged and another who is supported while he explores his interests and passions—will respond differently to life.

4. **Trauma in early childhood.** This last influence may be important to consider if you are raising a child who has been abused or neglected. You may have difficulty separating his innate character traits from those that have evolved out of fear of punishment. One adoptive father noticed his child's compulsion to clean or organize but recognized that his preference for keeping his room neat could either indicate the child's innate love for order or stem from fear. It is possible the child thought that he had been beaten for not keeping his room clean or mistakenly thought neatness would help him be more accepted. Since they were not sure what drove his neatness, this child's adoptive parents were careful not to focus too much praise on that behavior.

In a healthy home, a child's strongest traits generally will follow him from infancy through adulthood. Some kids truly do love to line up their things in organized ways, from their shoes to their toys! And those strong, innate traits are likely to impact both of you on a daily basis.

EFFECTS OF TRAITS

A child's strongest traits will affect:

- how he relates to other people,
- how he deals with problems,
- how he organizes his thoughts and carries out tasks, and
- what interests and motivates him.

In other words, becoming familiar with your child's personality will go a long way toward helping you understand why your child acts the way she does. No wonder scientists and philosophers have been trying to pin down the various temperaments for the last couple of millennia! While the ancient Greek physician Hippocrates is credited with identifying the four basic personality types (choleric, sanguine, melancholy, and phlegmatic), many others have fine-tuned those types into sixteen or more "personality clusters" since then. The idea of sixteen types makes my brain hurt, especially when assigned abbreviations like ESTP or INFJ.[1] Figuring out the alphabetical configuration for all five people in my own family reminds me of what happens at the crisis point in the children's book *Chicka Chicka Boom Boom* when all the alphabet letters crash into a big pile!

YOUR CHILD'S STRONG, INNATE TRAITS ARE LIKELY TO IMPACT BOTH OF YOU ON A DAILY BASIS.

PEGGING YOUR CHILD'S PERSONALITY

Is there any way to logically sort people into recognizable categories, and what is the value in that?

If the instructions in our genetic makeup could, as Dr. Paul Brand said, fill "a thousand six-hundred-page books," then it seems to me the human population must be a remarkably extensive library! Imagine a real library having no system whatsoever for sorting its hundreds of thousands of books. Can you imagine how difficult it would be to find a specific book in a library with no alphabetical system or category groupings?

Sorting books into even a few categories would help. A book of poetry could easily be distinguished from one on finance, for instance, simply by looking at the cover. Furthermore, a quick flip through the pages would reveal poetry stanzas rather than dollar signs and financial charts. Yet you wouldn't know much about what makes this book different from another book of poetry until you read it, right?

Personality typing works in much the same way. The more intimately you get to know a child, the more you will find that he cannot be stereotyped and summed up by one personality type. Yet children often reveal strengths and weaknesses in clusters that seem familiar. And familiarity can breed greater understanding.

One clear and creative approach to helping parents and kids identify their personality types is the children's book *The Treasure Tree*.[2] The book centers on the adventures of four animal characters: the Otter, the Beaver, the Golden Retriever, and the Lion, each of which possesses strong, very different character traits that correspond to the four basic personality types. The book tells how the four best friends must work together to reach a common goal (finding the four golden keys to the treasure tree). Without the Otter's enthusiasm, the Beaver's attention to detail, the Golden Retriever's sensitivity, and the Lion's leadership skills, the friends would not have been able to unlock the treasure. When I read the book to my preschool-age children, they were inspired to spontaneously assess and talk about their own personalities with some degree of insight.

Though many books on personality typing are available today, Hippocrates laid the foundation for subsequent discussions of personality when he identified the personality types nearly twenty-five hundred years ago. The four types and some of their commonly recognized characteristics are:

- Choleric: adventurous, determined, outspoken, competitive, strong-willed
- Sanguine: playful, sociable, talkative, lively, imaginative
- Melancholy: detailed, orderly, persistent, respectful, deep
- Phlegmatic: thoughtful, controlled, adaptable, attentive, diplomatic

Whether or not these terms are familiar to you, you've probably intuited a lot about your child's personality type just by noticing his everyday reactions and motivations. The quiz "Your Child's Got Personality!" will help you recognize what you may already know about your child and better understand why he behaves the way he does.

YOUR CHILD'S GOT PERSONALITY!

In some ways, determining your child's personality is an inexact science. She is likely a blend of more than one personality type, and as I noted earlier, a child's relationships and experiences also can influence the way she behaves. Still, it is helpful to get some sense of why your child acts the way she does. The following quiz, which is based on situations similar to those which you've already had—or will have—with your child, may help you identify your child's strongest traits.

1. You can truthfully say, "I'd be a millionaire if only I could bottle and sell my child's . . ."
   a. optimism.
   b. persistence.
   c. kindness.
   d. confidence.

2. Your son keeps you up until 2 a.m. the night before his school's science fair because
   a. though he's been talking for days about his great plans, he casually mentions over dinner that he hasn't actually started his project yet.
   b. he refuses to go to bed until you help him make sure that each planet in his model of the solar system is exactly to scale.
   c. he spent so much time helping his best friend finish *his* project that he's starting his own late.
   d. he's willing to sacrifice sleep in order to be sure his complicated and inno-vative project is better than anyone else's—and will win the blue ribbon.

3. When you take your daughter to her first overnight camp, you are impressed because she
   a. charms her counselor and makes five new friends before she's unpacked her bags.
   b. completes all five levels of the Red Cross swimming safety course in just one week.

c. is able to restore peace to her cabin after one camper unfairly accuses another of swiping a CD.

d. organizes and emcees the final night's camper talent show.

4. Your daughter comes home from school crying because

a. a boy drew laughs after school by mimicking her enthusiastic cheering during the previous day's football game.

b. despite carefully following all her teacher's detailed directions, she received a C on her art project.

c. she watched another child being mercilessly teased on the bus ride home and was unable to stop the bullies from picking on that classmate.

d. she lost her class's election for a seat on the student council.

5. When your child's teacher tells you how much she enjoys having your son in class, it is most likely because

a. he's creative, cheerful, and comes up with great new ideas.

b. he doesn't quit but keeps working on a project until it's done right.

c. he listens calmly and intently in class and does everything he can to please his teachers.

d. he catches on to material quickly and enjoys teaching other kids what he knows.

6. At age four, your child likes playing in the big sandbox at the park because

a. it is the best place to find a new friend to play with or someone else to talk to.

b. he loves to use his forty-eight-piece sand-castle kit to build intricate buildings.

c. he can see you sitting on the nearby bench at all times and knows you'll step in to help if an older child tries to steal his toys.

d. he has a captive audience and can tell everyone else what to build.

7. Your child's excuse for not cleaning her room on Saturday morning is that

a. she wants to tell you all about your neighbor's new puppy first.

b. there's nothing to clean. You walk in her room and find out she's right—everything is already clean and neatly organized.

c. she's unsure where to start.

d. she shouldn't have to clean her room until you start cleaning the rest of the house.

8. When you ask your child whether he'd like to return to your family's favorite vacation spot or take a sightseeing tour to New York City this summer, here is his reaction:

a. New York City! Maybe he'll actually run into celebrities when your family walks down Broadway. In fact, maybe one of them will even invite him to a casting call!

b. He'd prefer to return to the same resort, where he knows the schedule and what to expect each day of the week.

c. He'd choose your family's traditional spot; it holds warm memories for him.

d. He would pick New York City. It will be a new adventure, and he can already tell you the four sites your family must not miss.

9. Other people are always remarking on your child's

a. energy and enthusiasm.

b. attention to detail.

c. thoughtfulness.

d. leadership ability.

If you circled mostly *a*'s, your child is likely a sanguine and primarily interested in being with other people and having fun.

If you circled mostly *b*'s, your child is probably a melancholy who wants to get things just right.

If you circled mostly *c*'s, your child is most likely a phlegmatic who cares deeply about others' feelings.

If you circled mostly *d*'s, your child is probably a choleric who values adventure and being the leader.

Note: Many children have several characteristics from two of these types.

Even after completing this quiz, you may be unsure about your child's personality type. What if he possesses some traits that appear to be direct opposites? It's possible that your child is engaged in *activities* common to all personality types, which makes it a little difficult to discern what comes most naturally. How can you figure out whether behavior and activities are connected with inborn traits or whether your child has developed them to cope with others' expectations? Ask yourself (or your child) the following questions:

1. **What activities energize my child? drain her?** Think back to how your child spent last Saturday. Let's say that on this single day your daughter picked up her room, met with some fellow 4-H members to plan the group's next fundraiser, cheerfully entertained your friend's toddler while you and your friend visited, and then welcomed four of her closest friends to your house for a slumber party she'd spent weeks planning. Does that mean she's a melancholy, choleric, phlegmatic, and sanguine all rolled into one?

   No. Perhaps she picked up her toys only because you had made it clear that she must—and she really wants her allowance. She may be the one planning the fund-raiser because she really likes and wants to please the group's adviser. It's possible that she readily agreed to watch your friend's child because she thinks it will be so cool when she's old enough to babysit—and she had nothing fun planned that afternoon anyway.

   That evening, however, you noticed her eyes dancing with excitement as she waited for her friends to arrive. She chattered nonstop as she spread out the supplies for the craft project she'd planned. She hummed as she got out the snacks. When the doorbell rang, she ran to the door to welcome her first guest. After a busy day, she felt energized, excited, contented, more sanguine . . . more herself.

2. **What is the motivation behind engagement in those activities?** Priorities are often good indicators of inborn traits. Two kids who are interested in the same activity—say a sports camp—may sign up for very different reasons.

The first child excitedly registers but will stay in the camp only if her friend signs up too. She thinks, *After all, what fun can it possibly be without friends?*

The second child eagerly signs up for the same camp. But when asked by his mother if he'd like his best friend to sign up with him, he responds, "Um, no, not this time." Why not? Because he is determined to learn the sport itself. He's concerned that his playful, exuberant friend might distract him. He thinks, *After all, what fun can it be to go to a sports camp and not learn the sport?* He'd rather arrange another time to play with his friend.

As you can see, the first child's priority is nurturing relationships. A person who tends to be social, animated, bouncy, enthusiastic, funny, and highly extroverted is likely to be energized by people and truly dislike being alone. Activity choices revolve around who to get together with and when.

The second child's priority is goal mastery. Some children love to plan and achieve goals. *That* is what energizes and excites them. It doesn't mean the second child is not sociable; his priorities are simply different.

3. **Is it more valuable, perhaps, to define what my child is not, rather than what he is? Will that at least eliminate activities that drain and unmotivate?** Sometimes it may be more clear what a person is *not* than what he is. Let's say you inwardly cringe each time you notice your ten-year-old son's messy, bulging backpack. It's jammed with dog-eared textbooks, old homework assignments, outdated notices from school—even leftovers from last week's lunches. You constantly urge him to clean it out— and on occasion even do so yourself—only to feel your irritation rise a few days later when you stumble over the stuffed backpack that he's left lying in the hallway again. Clearly, neatness and organization are not his strengths.

Yet this same son may excel at playing the trumpet. He carefully guards his prized instrument and, in addition to practicing for band class, enjoys improvising new melodies. Because of the way your son motivates and entertains his fellow band members, the band teacher considers him a prize student and natural leader.

Let's say that same band teacher is the student council adviser and encourages your son to run for a spot in student government. While it might not make much sense for your son to serve as secretary or treasurer—who knows what would happen to the notes or money entrusted to him?—his leadership skills might make him an excellent president or class representative. Discerning your child's weaknesses from his strengths can assist you as you help him choose activities. That doesn't mean you won't encourage him to edge out of his comfort zone once in a while, but you'll know better when to let things be.

4. **Even with a good idea of what energizes and motivates my child, could I jump to conclusions that might not be accurate?** Sometimes our own desires for our children cause us to overfocus on strengths that we think will prove most useful to a child. What you see as the main course in your child (his major strengths or gifts) may indeed only be side dishes (minor strengths).

LISTEN TO YOUR CHILD AS HE EXPRESSES WHAT DOES AND DOES NOT INTEREST HIM.

One classic example, replayed endlessly in movies, is that of the formerly athletic dad who hopes to live out his own failed dreams through his child. He's optimistic about and perhaps exaggerates potential in his child's couple of home runs, only to realize later with chagrin that his son prefers the arts to sports.

An obvious way to avoid this pitfall is to listen to your child as he expresses what does and does not interest him. That doesn't mean you never push a child to try something he's not immediately interested in—a reluctant soccer player may indeed end up loving it (though he won't necessarily want to devote excess time to it).

As my son has grown up, I've made honest attempts to listen to his desires and review his strengths along the way. I can still remember the day I cuddled with four-year-old Tyler as we read *The Treasure Tree.* At that time, he immediately recognized the Lion and Beaver in himself—he's always loved to categorize things.

Recently, to help Tyler figure out what he wants to be "when he grows up" (or at least what to study in college next year), a career counselor gave Tyler an objective set of tests on career interests, personality, study skills, etc. I was *extremely* curious to find out whether this counselor—who had never met my son or talked to me about him—might see in raw scores the strengths I'd observed in Tyler since he was three years old!

Had my studies of personality since he was small truly helped me recognize his strengths? Or had it all been filtered through my own imagination and dreams for him?

When Tyler got the results of his tests back—his answers compiled into a profile with the counselor's insights about his personality—my son said, "Wow! This guy must be a mind reader!"

Of course the counselor is not. Tyler had simply revealed plenty about himself through his answers to hundreds of questions—including his attitudes toward leadership, work environments, and even God.

So were the counselor's conclusions the same as my own?

Yes and no.

For one, I realized that my assumptions about Tyler's interests had been too influenced by my familiarity with his academic record (which the career counselor never saw). Despite the many upper level science and math classes that Tyler had chosen to take in high school, he hadn't marked on the interest questionnaires anything related to science or math. His interest in flying airplanes fit his profile well, but the counselor also suggested he might be suited for a business career.

Business? What? Hmmm. Then I remembered his negotiation skills (remember the cookies before dinner?). Furthermore, the test results suggest that Tyler will never be happy confined to a desk or lab.

Several months later, he has decided to study flight technology, which offers excitement and flexibility, while using his math and mechanical reasoning strengths in a more subconscious way.

In the long run, our personalities may have more of an affect on career choice than our intellectual capabilities. No matter how well you get to know your kids, beware of pigeonholing them. They will still surprise you!

HURRAY FOR DIVERSITY

It's a good thing we are designed with such differences! The human population needs variety. Romans 12:4-5 describes the need for different gifts within the church:

Just as each of us has one body with many members, and these members do not all have the same function, so in Christ we who are many form one body, and each member belongs to all the others. If you have ever found yourself embarrassed or let down by your child's personality, remember that God designed your child with a particular temperament for a reason! You, as the parent, have the incredible privilege of seeing how those traits are used to strengthen your family, as well as your child's school, friendships, and, eventually, your child's life work.

Now that you've had an opportunity to consider your child's leanings, next up is an examination of how traits can cause friction between children and their parents. As we focus on when "differences" means "difficulties," I hope you will continue to remember all that is admirable and worthy of praise in your child.

5

CLASH AND BURN

This is Olivia.
She is good at lots of things.
She is very good at wearing people out.

THE OPENING LINES FROM IAN FALCONER'S CHILDREN'S BOOK *OLIVIA*[1]

Just like Olivia, the energetic, adorable piglet in Falconer's children's picture book, little Shari was a ball of energy, but less controlled. In elementary school, Shari was moved to the front row of the classroom so she could focus, then to the back of the room so everyone else could. Her teachers constantly admonished her. "Sit down." "Be quiet!" At home, to release energy, she set a pillow on the floor, placed her head on it, and ran circles around herself.

Now an adult, Shari is still circling and talking—but it's around the country, by plane, when she's hired by school administrators to "Please, stand up!" and "Speak!" The child whom professionals assessed in first grade and predicted would never get past the fifth grade now has her graduate degree in education. Her gifted speaking inspires children, women's groups, and corporate audiences.[2]

Dr. Mel Levine, a learning disabilities expert, writes, "Sometimes the very same traits that jeopardize your kid in third grade could evolve into his prize assets during adulthood. Distractibility and daydreaming during reading class may be an attention deficit yet may also be early indicators of creativity and innovative thinking, 'symptoms' that will bolster her career as a scriptwriter or music video producer."[3]

SOMETIMES BEHAVIORAL DIFFICULTIES ARE BASED ON A CHILD'S PERSONALITY AND SETTING: WHO A CHILD IS WITH AND WHAT THE EXPECTATIONS ARE.

Some traits are certainly related to a neurological dysfunction, which we'll consider in the next chapter. But sometimes difficulties are based primarily on a child's personality and the setting: who a child is with and what the expectations are. Sometimes the only problem is that personalities clash: your child's with his siblings', his friends', his teacher's, or your own!

In the first half of this chapter, I'll explore some difficulties that arise from personality differences. In the second half, I'll offer some tips on how to deal with these issues. You see, increased understanding of those dynamics can help you anticipate and better deal with potential conflicts. It can help you learn to be more patient and help you delight more in your child.

WHEN DIFFERENCES CAN LEAD TO DIFFICULTIES

Have you ever felt a sudden flash of annoyance when your child's behavior doesn't match your expectations? Perhaps she looks down and says nothing when a friend of yours greets her. He may wander off as you look at paint samples in the hardware store. Maybe she giggles during the entire theater performance. At such moments, you may not enjoy being with your child very much. Yet simply understanding the source of your irritation can go a long way in helping you overcome frustration and correct your child effectively. The first step is realizing that personality clashes can occur when:

- opposite personalities conflict
- similar personalities annoy one another
- behavior doesn't meet expectations or suit specific environments (say Grandma's condo or a rigid classroom)
- an adult feels extra responsible for controlling a child
- stress exaggerates strong traits

Opposites Don't Always Attract

"You like potato and I like po-tah-to / You like tomato and I like to-mah-to. . . ." That old Gershwin song ("Let's Call the Whole Thing Off") reminds me of how different we can be from our kids. Not that most parents really want to call the whole thing off, but even the most dedicated become frustrated during those moments when parenting is not quite what they bargained for.

You may not always be patient with your child when she displays inherent personality traits, especially if they are directly opposite from your own. If you are quiet by nature, a nonstop chatterer may annoy you, no matter how much you love your child. Conversely, if you are sociable, you may lose patience with a shy, quiet thinker who has trouble expressing feelings and thoughts. A child with a strong inborn sense of fairness coupled with a strong will may want to debate every issue. That may drive you nuts—especially when half the time he is right.

Drs. Stella Chess and Alexander Thomas first explored how a number of inborn temperamental traits affect the "goodness of fit" in parent-child relationships.[4] Consider how you and your child differ in terms of persistence and attention span, activity level, sensory threshold, mood and intensity of responses, approach or withdrawal, adaptability, and regularity. It's easy to see how problems can arise if you and your child differ in these areas. Perhaps you can relate to one of the following examples.

Persistence and attention span: You want to hurry to the grocery store. Your child slowly and deliberately insists on tying his own shoes, wait, just let him make that loop . . . very slowly . . . then, oops . . . start over. Or you want your child to stick with and finish the project she insisted you do together, and now she's wandering, daydreaming, already clamoring to do something else.

Activity level: You are exhausted from work and want to relax and read *Winnie the Pooh* to your child. He wants to roller skate, hike, bike, go, go, go! If you're the one with a high activity level, you may spend an entire morning fruitlessly searching for the perfect outfit for your daughter to wear in an upcoming family portrait. When you tell her you're willing to drive to another mall to continue the search, she may burst into tears and say she just wants to go home.

Sensory threshold: You barely notice sounds, smells, or the textures of fabrics. She incessantly overreacts to neck tags and other such dreadful stuff. You think she's hysterical. She thinks you're insensitive. Or maybe your child drives you crazy by making loud truck noises as he pushes his monster truck across the kitchen floor while you're at the table trying to balance your family's budget.

Mood and intensity of responses: You are emotionally expressive. He's hard to read. Getting him to tell you what's going on in his mind is like pulling teeth. Or perhaps your child becomes hysterical over a scratch that doesn't even bleed, and you want to say, "Just get *over* it!"

Approach or withdrawal: You are outgoing and the life of every party. You've got to drop your child off at preschool and run some errands, but your child is shyly, stubbornly clinging to you. Or you may be a little shy and your child charges up to strangers, forcing you to interact with them when you may not feel entirely comfortable doing so.

Adaptability: You've set aside a day to swim and play at a new water park on your family vacation. When you pull off the interstate and into the newly paved parking lot, however, you discover that the park hasn't officially opened yet. Though you're all disappointed, you can't understand why your son is still sulking late that afternoon while the rest of the family is having a blast building an ornate sand castle at the nearby public beach. If your child is the more adaptable one, however, he may be the one to suggest going to the beach while you're angrily composing a letter in your head to the magazine that said the water park had opened the previous week.

Regularity: A friend calls and invites you to the mall for lunch. Frustrated, you tell her no. Though you'd love to go, you know that if your toddler daughter doesn't eat or sleep at exactly the same time every day she becomes an emotional mess. Perhaps it is *you* who likes predictability. Just when you get used to working during his naps he changes his schedule again. Then he quits napping altogether and you wring your hands. When will you ever get your work done?

"You like potato and I like po-tah-to. . . ." Can you see how personality differences can lead to big conflicts with your child? As I'll point out over and over again, just being aware of how your personality traits are different—as well as alike—can help you maintain your cool.

Two Peas in a Pod

What about when you and your child share traits? While it is typically easier to understand a child who is like you, similarities in personality can create their own set of problems. If you are aware of shared traits, you may feel mixed emotions when your child displays weaknesses you struggled with as a child, such as stubbornness or impulsivity. Your heart may be in the right place—you want to prevent your child from making similar mistakes—but beware of overexaggerating a particular weakness and unfairly labeling her. Remember, she is not you, and you are not her. Telling her "You are just as stubborn as I was as a kid, and boy did that get me in trouble!" may not be helpful.

On the other hand, you may unconsciously share a trait with your child and then wonder why you have so much conflict. Remember that two strong-willed people can butt heads like mountain goats. Two talkers may argue endlessly. Two flighty people may distract each other.

Class Conformity

Sometimes your child's personality causes conflict with people outside your family. In a group setting, such as a classroom, all members are often expected to cooperate in the same way. A high energy, distractible child can complicate life for his teacher, who may be trying to engage an entire group of children in a math lesson.

It can unnerve her when one kid, in constant motion and need of redirection, gets all the other children off track. After all, that teacher is responsible for the care and education of the entire group! Anything that threatens her ability to do that well can be disconcerting or frustrating, especially if she herself tends to be sensitive to noise or movement or is easily distracted.

BEING AWARE OF HOW THE PERSONALITY TRAITS OF YOU AND YOUR CHILD ARE DIFFERENT— AS WELL AS ALIKE—CAN HELP YOU MAINTAIN YOUR COOL.

Dr. Mel Levine, who wrote about learning differences in *A Mind at a Time,* notes that parents and teachers tend to expect students to excel in every area:

> Every day [students] are expected to shine in math, reading, writing, speaking, spelling, memorization, comprehension, problem solving, socialization, athletics, and following verbal directions. Few if any children can master all of these "trades." And none of us adults can.

In one way or another, all minds have their specialties and their frailties.[5]

But even a teacher who agrees with this principle is still responsible for ensuring that her entire class passes the math section of the next standardized test or keeping a group of preschoolers together during circle time. A kid who is different from the rest of the crowd may create a frustrating learning environment for himself, his teacher, and his fellow students. However, if he is placed in an environment that better matches his learning style, his frustration is likely to decrease or even end.[6]

You're Not in Kansas Anymore

You may have different expectations for your child when you're away from home. When a little whirlwind visits relatives, she risks breaking Grandma's favorite vase. If she jumps across the floor of her aunt's upstairs apartment, she may risk annoying the downstairs neighbors when their ceiling starts shaking.

Sometimes issues are only issues in context. My child Elisa's personal motto, "Why walk when you can jump?" creates no problem in our own home and goes largely unnoticed except when she wants to jump down stairs five at a time instead of two. (I was tremendously relieved when at four years old she saw a flight of about ten steep stairs and wisely said, "I'm not gonna jump down those.") But whenever we stay overnight in a hotel room, my husband and I are suddenly sensitive to every little leap and stomp. After all, it's our responsibility to be sure other people aren't disturbed. I turn into a nag.

At home, a child's constant motion and chatter can distract Mom or Dad from getting tasks done. Even if Mom eventually gives up trying to balance the checkbook so she can take her youngster to the park to burn energy, she's likely to feel she's shirking her duties. But in reality, helping her daughter find an acceptable outlet for her energy is Mom's responsibility. Understanding the source of frustration can go a long way in helping Mom do that.

Stress Magnets

When a child is stressed, his strongest character traits tend to be magnified. When a child picks up tension in the household, revealed by his parents' increased nagging, a rushed schedule, or expressions of anger or tears, he is likely to react in a way that gets their attention.

A sensitive child will become more hysterical (or more withdrawn) than usual. An active child may become even busier, perhaps even acting out of control; a strong-willed child will likely become more defiant. Again, understanding that your child is simply reacting to the environment rather than setting out to annoy you may help you better cope with and address unwanted behavior.

WHEN A CHILD IS STRESSED, HIS STRONGEST CHARACTER TRAITS TEND TO BE MAGNIFIED.

Increased Responsibility = Increased Frustration

High-energy and overreactive kids are often difficult for adults to handle simply because their caretakers feel the burden of assuming *extra* responsibility to keep these kids from harming themselves or others. For instance, hyperactivity and clumsiness in a child can make for a dangerous mix, turning observers into nervous wrecks.

Can you relate to the embarrassment Susan Martins Miller describes below?

> Being out in public can be difficult just because you can never be sure what your child will do. If you tell your son or daughter to stay close to you in the grocery store—a reasonable request made by most parents— there may be an explosion right there in the middle of the produce aisle. As other shoppers steer their carts around the screaming kid thrashing around on the floor demanding fruit snacks, you feel dozens of eyes looking at you. Silently you wonder why you cannot control your child. Then the mother of four well-behaved adorable children rolls by, calmly pulling items off the shelf in a family atmosphere of sweet cooperation. And you ask yourself, "Why doesn't my kid sit still in the cart like that? Is it too much to expect I might buy groceries without a major incident?"[7]

Although most parents don't have to deal with this on every trip to the store, most children throw a fit at some point. Such tantrums are especially common among kids who are assertive, sensitive, and struggle with transitions and verbal expression of feelings. Of course a hungry or tired toddler or preschooler may blow at any time as well!

But the reality is that many parents *do* experience struggles like this on a day-to-day basis. They feel guilty that they don't always like their children—although they do love them. Such children may eventually mellow and find better ways to deal with energy or feelings of sensitivity or frustration. In other words, they may lose the need for other people to control and take responsibility for them as they do this for themselves. Again, just taking the long view may help parents cope in the meantime.

Want some additional tips for dealing with personality clashes between you and your children?

1. **Focus on the positives.** How can you keep the proper perspective when your child is driving you nuts? Take a moment to consider the advice of Philippians 4:8: "Whatever is true, whatever is noble, whatever is right, whatever is pure, whatever is lovely, whatever is admirable—if anything is excellent or praiseworthy—think about such things."

   What in your child *is* excellent, honorable, and admirable? How often do you fix your thoughts on what is lovely and worthy of praise? That same child who always seems to defy you may someday be able to look a classmate in the eye and say "No!" when he's offered a joint. Your extremely shy daughter may be the only one with enough sensitivity to reach the lonely heart of a grandparent who is grieving over the loss of a spouse.

   It can be refreshing to stop, look at your kids, and listen

WHAT IN YOUR CHILD *IS* EXCELLENT, WORTHY OF PRAISE, HONORABLE, AND ADMIRABLE? HOW OFTEN DO YOU FIX YOUR THOUGHTS ON THE POSITIVES?

to them long enough and deeply enough to consider all that is admirable in them. Delight in those attributes you see, in any measure!

2. **Consider positive sides of "negative" traits, and share those with other grown-ups who spend time with your child.** Sometimes finding the positive means looking at an annoying trait in a new way. You may be frustrated when your child wanders away five minutes after starting to paint (and after you spent twice that long locating and dragging out all the supplies), but don't forget the bright side: Your easily distracted child is also likely to be flexible. That means that if you read about a fun family event in the paper, only to discover it starts in fifteen minutes, you and your child might actually make it there on time. Also, a flexible child may gracefully let you stop in the middle of a table game that you find dull.

An extremely stubborn child may frustrate you by insisting on dressing himself in a striped shirt and plaid shorts. Don't forget, however, that he will also—before you know it—efficiently pack a school backpack without a whit of supervision.

When my daughter Elisa was two, she often became terribly upset when adults laughed at her cute little waddle or way of talking. She would run off to her room and hide, leaving well-meaning visitors feeling puzzled and concerned. I usually told them, "Don't sweat it. That's just her way—she'll get over it!" After a while, she did.

With maturity, Elisa's sensitivity has turned primarily

outward. For the last two years, she has been unable to hear an ambulance siren without dropping everything to pray for its occupants. Imagine being injured and upset, lying in a racing ambulance with its lights flashing and sirens sounding. Meanwhile, a small child within earshot literally drops to her knees—right smack in the middle of a playdate—asking God to help *you!*

3. **Be honest with your child about differences.** Your child is also likely to react more positively if he understands your differences and how they sometimes lead to conflict. Don't just point out your differences, however; be sure to tell your child what you appreciate about him. For example, say "I can appreciate that you are [energetic, sensitive . . .]. That's a good thing and will help you [accomplish your goals, make others feel cared for . . .]. I am different from you in that I like to [relax when I get home, be flexible . . .], and that can be a good thing too."

4. Don't pigeonhole your child. Never assume you have your child all figured out. In the next chapter, we'll talk about using labels to help diagnose children with disabilities. Personality typing is a form of labeling as well. Behaviors are clustered together, and kids with those personalities are assumed to act exactly alike. That isn't so—kids are also affected by their experiences and their own special wiring.

5. **Learn to compromise, and teach your child to do the same.** For example, if your child hates sudden transitions,

build into your mental schedule a little extra time for five-minute warnings to wrap up activities. If your activity level is higher than your child's, be willing to spend less time doing what you want to avoid burning out your child.

By the same token, talk to your child about making "trades": "Stick with me without complaining until I can get these errands done, then we'll stop at a fast-food joint with an indoor playground where you can run like crazy."

6. **Accept that parenting requires some self-sacrifice, but take breaks when you need them.** If your child requires more energy to parent than others, you're probably well versed in the sacrifices of parenthood! Don't forget, however, that you need time to recharge. That may mean asking your spouse or a friend to help so you can spend some time away from your child.

Keep tabs on your own emotional meter. If you have PMS, overdue bills, and you didn't sleep much last night because a child woke up twice in pain from an ear infection, it won't take much to make you impatient or annoyed or weepy. Forgive yourself if you overreact, and recognize when you need time alone.

If the conflicts between you and your child ever increase your anger to the point that you may be abusive (including verbally), it's critical that you get help and find some new strategies.

7. **Get help from other family members who share traits with your child.** It may seem like a no-brainer to suggest

that family members with like interests do things together, but it's possible they may need a suggestion or a reminder. It's likely, however, that the more they have fun together, the more they will cook up activities on their own. A few suggestions for Gordy to take Elisa outdoors while I worked at home blossomed into countless trips they've taken together to hike, bike, kayak, skate, and rock climb.

8. **Use appendix A to find additional resources** that will offer you specific strategies relating to your child's strongest personality traits. Consider this book a bit like your travel agency as you begin your quest to get to know your child, offering a map to point you in the right direction and suggesting some stops along the way. For instance, if you're traveling through life with an extremely strong-willed child, I recommend the book *You Can't Make Me (But I Can Be Persuaded)* by Cynthia Tobias. You can also find parenting groups listed in appendix A.

Personality clashes are often the source of frustration between parent and child. Occasionally, however, a hidden disability is the cause of a child's baffling behavior. If you suspect your child may have a disability, how can you uncover it? How can you help a child struggling with a disability? Finally, how can you delight in your child in the midst of the added challenges that disabilities bring? Those are the questions we'll consider in the next chapter.

6

DISABILITY DILEMMAS

Each kid unrolls an original mural of mind traits.
The challenge is to understand his or her special wiring and its implications
for parenting, counseling, and educating.

MEL LEVINE, M.D., *A MIND AT A TIME*[1]

When a flight attendant I met on a business trip learned that I'm a parenting author, she described a concern she had about her toddler. She said he had been walking *very* strangely. She demonstrated the weird gait he had adopted and frequently used, marching bowlegged, lifting his knees high. Why on earth would he do that?

I burst out laughing. Fortunately, not one hour before, she'd told me how much her toddler loved the movie *Mary Poppins* and watched it repeatedly.

I asked, "So . . . isn't he just doing 'Step in Time'?" The exact title of the song was fuzzy to me, but I hummed the tune and reminded her how Dick Van Dyke had been cast as a sooty chimney sweep, dancing across the rooftops. She looked startled, then laughed too.

"That *must* be it! Oh, I need to call my husband to let him know the mystery is solved!"

If you've ever experienced that nagging fear that something isn't quite right with your child, you will understand this mother's relief. Unfortunately, not all strange behaviors can be so easily pinned down to Disney-itis, and not all our worries can be cast aside so easily.

In the last chapter, we explored how personality clashes can dampen delight. If your child's behavior perplexes or irritates you, first consider whether his actions stem from a particular personality trait. Sometimes, however, a problem behavior or developmental delay is related to a disability. Pinpointing such a problem can help relieve the frustration felt by both parent and child.

QUESTIONS TO ASK

Elaine sensed that something wasn't quite right with her first baby.[2] Andrea didn't make eye contact as her mother thought an infant probably should. But it wasn't until Elaine had her second child that she was convinced that her firstborn struggled in many ways that other kids didn't, including difficulties with large motor skills.

In preschool, Andrea behaved differently in some ways from her peers. Those behaviors were neither extreme nor disruptive. They were simply off-kilter, odd enough to confuse her peers and their mothers, causing a few to wonder what caused Andrea's struggles and whether it was related to a disability.

When you see differences in your child that are unexplainable, one or more questions should cross your mind before you ever consider a diagnostic label:

1. **Is she just going through a phase?** For instance, you might wonder if your child's tantrums are age appropriate. If he's a toddler or approaching adolescence, you probably can neatly file that annoying—yet probably temporary— behavior under the label "Terrible Twos" or "Temperamental Teens."

   This doesn't make tantrums much easier to endure, but at least you know relief will come. Tips from other mothers can help defuse your anger and frustration. Also, understanding your child's personality type can help you determine his emotional limits.

2. **Was he born this way, or has he been mishandled or injured?** If your child's behavior is troubling and you can't determine its cause, think about how you have been disciplining him. Is your approach consistent and confident, yet fair and loving? If not, your child may respond inappropriately.

   Sometimes a parent's anger can even lead to abuse. If you ever feel out of control when disciplining your child, do both you and your son or daughter a favor and seek help. If you suspect your child is being abused by someone else, be aware that abused children are often withdrawn, extremely self-critical, and quiet. Inappropriate sexual behavior, of course, often signals sexual abuse. Not surprisingly, foster children and those adopted after infancy are more likely to display signs of abuse.

3. **Does my child have a disability?** If behavior or developmental delays cannot be explained by personality, disciplinary methods, or abuse, or if a child obviously struggles in ways that her peers do not, a disability may be responsible. It could be caused by genetics, improper growth and development in the womb, or birth trauma.

You may wonder if your son is just a slow learner who will eventually catch up, or if delays will hold him back indefinitely if he doesn't receive help. By all means, consider testing.

Elaine's daughter, Andrea, is a beautiful child with a winning smile. She is obviously bright, even intellectually advanced in some ways. But people noticed early on that Andrea would flap her hands whenever she became excited, and she sometimes walked awkwardly, on tiptoes. The monkey bars and other equipment on the preschool playground presented a tremendous physical challenge for her.

Even more worrisome to Elaine were Andrea's struggles in connecting with other kids at times. Conversations felt stilted and disjointed in a way that was difficult to pinpoint. Andrea obviously wanted to engage in conversations with other kids and to be like them. But to try and be like them, she often literally imitated them . . . which didn't always go over well. Andrea's behavior and development were so obviously different from her peers' and younger sister's that her parents

DO YOU SUSPECT A DISABILITY?

Are you concerned about your child's

- lack of short-term or long-term memory?
- inability to focus attention?
- struggle to understand spoken or written language or to express himself clearly and age-appropriately?
- inability to figure things out on her own, organize her thinking, or understand a sequence of events?
- difficulty interacting age-appropriately with other kids or adults?
- struggles with fine motor skills (e.g., handwriting) or eye-hand coordination (e.g., cutting with scissors)?
- physical awkwardness on the playground, or lack of balance?
- overreactions or underreactions to sounds, smells, textures, or a busy visual environment?

If so, consider having your child assessed by a pediatrician or a team of occupational, physical, and/or speech therapists who may be able to help him be more successful.

decided to have her tested. At a children's hospital, a doctor diagnosed her with mild Asperger's Syndrome, a term for borderline autism that includes socialization struggles.

Though relieved to be able to put a name to Andrea's unusual behavior, her parents remained concerned. The word *autism,* which is connected to Asperger's Syndrome, can be quite frightening.

Also, Andrea's symptoms didn't match the syndrome exactly. Unlike typical kids with Asperger's, Andrea could offer give-and-take in conversations. That was one reason her parents wondered whether educators had simply given Andrea the diagnosis du jour.

WHAT'S WRONG WITH YOUR CHILD?

Before making a diagnosis, pediatricians or psychologists and therapists (speech and language therapists, occupational therapists, physical therapists, etc.) ask questions about and observe a child's motor, mental, and social skills. Generally they consider both parents' impressions of how their child responds. Ideally, they should also observe a child in several different environments. They contrast a child with other children they have worked with and studied, and they interpret scores from tests they deem professionally reliable.

Unless a parent does an exceptional job of providing details of a child's day-to-day living to doctors and therapists, these professionals draw their conclusions primarily from what is seen and recorded during testing. The pediatrician, therapist, or teacher assessing your child's attention span, for instance, does not see him at home, focusing on his favorite TV show, nor does he or she see him in the morning having a meltdown when trying to tie his shoes.

The odds are high that with a thorough assessment, these professionals can suggest the *most likely* diagnosis. It's simply important to keep in mind that unlike Down syndrome, which can be determined genetically, diagnoses of disabilities such as learning disabilities, autism, and mood disorders are really highly educated guesses.

For example, a fairly commonly diagnosed condition today is attention deficit hyperactivity disorder, or ADHD. It's estimated that 3 to 5 percent, or 2 million children and adolescents in the United States, have attention deficit hyperactivity disorder.[3] Many parents are relieved by a diagnosis, because identifying the source of a child's distractibility and hyperactivity makes it seem somehow more manageable, less mysterious. But it's important to realize the "diagnosis" of a learning disability (as opposed to a known physical disability) is based on *patterns of behavior* or evidences of skill levels. Again, it is an imperfect science.

DIAGNOSES OF DISABILITIES SUCH AS LEARNING DISABILITIES, AUTISM, AND MOOD DISORDERS ARE REALLY HIGHLY EDUCATED GUESSES.

Remember what Edison said about his mother? Reading between the lines, I began to wonder: *What in him tried his mother's patience? How was he a "careless boy"?* The word *careless* brings to mind behaviors that often cause exasperated parents or teachers to give up too easily on kids. In fact, Edison's teachers did. Yet his mother and sister obviously believed in and nurtured him.

Now Edison has been labeled by some parents "the ADD Poster Child" to give hope to parents of kids who struggle with attention deficits. But I wonder: If little boy Edison were alive today, would that label help or hinder? Would he be plugged into a special education program with his own personal IEP (Individualized Education Plan) because his low standardized test scores—contrasted with amazingly high IQ scores—suggest a learning disability?

Would little Edison's carelessness (or perhaps inattentiveness to that which bores him) prevent him from qualifying for gifted education . . . deeming him, what then, *un*gifted?

THE HAZARDS OF LABELING YOUR CHILD

Labels are sometimes slapped on children too quickly by parents or professionals to conveniently explain away unusual behaviors, personalities, or abilities. They may prevent us from looking deeper to discern a child's unique gifts and strengths. Overfocusing on negative labels can steal joy from parenting.

Unnecessary labeling may occur when a child's strong personality traits are misunderstood or when a student's learning environment doesn't accommodate his style.

A child who, in a fairly rigid and controlling class, is less calm and more distractible than the average kid (or gets in trouble frequently) may erroneously be assumed to have a disability. Medication may be suggested "just in case" to help him act more "normal."

While medications often do help many children focus their attention better, leading to increased academic success and increased cooperation with adults, some kids are labeled before the influence of personality traits and environment are properly considered.

Too-quick typecasting occurs when a label or diagnosis is applied to a child with insufficient information. At its worst, a child may be prescribed inappropriate medication. For instance, one drug commonly used for attention deficit may aggravate bipolar disorder.[4] Wrong labels may also lead school staff to place a child in a learning environment that doesn't fit his needs—or even exaggerates problems.

Sometimes a parent may want to limit the number of school staff members who are privy to a child's diagnosis, especially a best-guess diagnosis. A parent may rightly fear that some (especially staff who won't have the opportunity to closely get to know the child) might develop a bias against her or have low expectations for her. It may be helpful to tell a child's teacher about a diagnosis, but sometimes it is best to allow the teacher and child time to get to know one another so the teacher doesn't make snap judgments. However, if problems are obvious from the start and a teacher's ability to help the child is compromised by not knowing about a diagnosis, then it may be best to be open from the first day of school, if not before. Once a diagnosis is shared, Mom and Dad should ask about confidentiality rules at their child's school to find out who will be given information and why.

Malicious name-calling, jokes, or sarcasm always hurt. Comments like "Hey, brain!" or "Aren't you in *special* class?" sting. Many kids, when they discover anything whatsoever different about another child, attach a hurtful label or nickname to their classmate. Yet fear of this should never prevent parents from trying to get to the bottom of their child's struggles. And fortunately or unfortunately, as labeling becomes more common, kids who need special help seem to stand out less than in years past. It is wise, however, to find out how kids who receive special services are transitioned in and out of the classroom (or helped within the classroom); ideally this is done in ways that don't call unnecessary attention to the child.

Judgmental or thoughtless comments from adults can hurt as well. "He's really hyper, isn't he?" one adult may say to another in front of a child.

If this happens to you, give people the benefit of the doubt. If you aren't sure what they mean, ask rather than assuming they are being judgmental. Smile and say, "He is busy, isn't he? Fortunately he's got about the same energy as most kids." Or, "Yeah, I wish I had that kind of energy sometimes, don't you?"

If your child is truly disabled by hyperactivity or another condition, admit that it is exhausting. If you are exploring ways to help him, you might mention that, while also mentioning how you enjoy some of your child's strengths (especially if the conversation has occurred within earshot of your child). "You should see how she channels that energy into her artwork! I'd love to show you one of her latest creations."

Of course, when others make a deliberately insensitive or critical comment that wounds you or your child, you may feel sick at heart. Instead of dwelling on such a remark, you may need to take a deep breath and simply choose to forgive those people. Pray for increased sensitivity on their part. If you fear that they may hurt other children in the same way, you may choose to speak directly with them. Pray for confidence and the ability to address the issue in a Christlike manner.

Sibling comparisons—even well-intended compliments—made in front of the kids can cause problems as well.[5]

For instance, frequent identification of one child as the "organized" one and the other as "disorganized" will cause problems. The one deemed organized may eventually feel resentful of that constant expectation, or she may feel superior to her sibling. The other may excuse his sloppy behavior with a shrug, saying, "Oh well! That's just me—the disorganized one."

Let your kids know that along with individual strengths come weaknesses. Those weaknesses can, however, be tempered or tamed. And there can be too much of a good thing (for instance, perfectionism). Remind siblings of each other's strengths and talk about creative ways to help each other.

Focusing on weaknesses without emphasizing strengths may cause a child to overidentify with his label and struggle with a poor self-image. Yes, you want to help him, but sometimes talking about a disability too much can be counterproductive.

Too broad assumptions about what a child is or is not capable of (by teachers, coaches, or even parents) may prevent a child from being encouraged to reach his full potential. By remaining a vocal, active parent who points out your child's strengths and accomplishments, you may be able to prevent stereotypical thinking.

THE HELPFULNESS OF LABELING YOUR CHILD

Labels *can* be useful when they help parents recognize common clusters of traits, abilities, or disabilities. They can be used as tools to guide parents to information and support.

Also, what helps one child with specific attributes or struggles may help another with similar struggles. Identifying specific problem areas can help a child realize with relief that he's not the only kid who moves, thinks, or feels the way he does. It can reassure Mom and Dad as well.

LABELS *CAN* BE USEFUL WHEN THEY SERVE AS TOOLS TO GUIDE PARENTS TO INFORMATION AND SUPPORT.

The good news for Andrea is that her diagnosis got her some help at a time she needed it. Short-term speech therapy and an extra year of preschool—in a pre-K class—gave her time and assistance in practicing socialization skills. To help her practice motor skills and enjoy a family activity at the same time, her dad often took her swimming. To have ignored Andrea's struggles would not have made them go away, and her parents have a continued awareness of where she needs help. Some of those needs are related to her personality and some to her unique physical and social struggles, which have diminished as she has matured.

Parents and their children may feel relief when they finally understand not only the source of the child's struggles, but how it may be treated. Of course, a label (especially a medical diagnosis or a severe learning disability) can be very upsetting. It may suggest that a child will experience lifelong challenges, and a parent is likely to proceed throughout the stages of grief: from denial and anger to acceptance of their child's disability.

Parents of a child with a disabling mental handicap realize their child may never grow up in the same sense that other children do. The grief and burden of responsibility may feel very heavy.

Yet there can be some relief in finally attaching a name to something that was formerly elusive. Mom and Dad are reassured to know that their child's unusual behaviors were not imagined and that some other kids struggle with the same thing. And when difficult behavior is treated effectively, the child's positive attributes are more likely to shine.

SOME CHILDREN FEEL STIGMATIZED BY LABELS. OTHERS ARE SIMPLY GLAD TO FIND OUT THEY AREN'T

It can also bring some comfort to a child who knows himself that something *is* wrong, but when *not* acknowledged made him feel "stupid" or "bad." Several adults have told me that they had a terrible time in school and only recently realized they had—and some still have—learning disabilities. They wish they had known that LD kids usually possess average to above average intelligence.

Some children feel stigmatized by labels. Others are simply glad to find out they aren't stupid after all. In the process of testing, they may discover multiple strengths, even gifts, and may learn to say, "I'm very good at W, X, and Y but sometimes need help with Z."

When a disability is hidden or when a child has strange symptoms that could be personality related (but may not be), his parents often don't get much support. One mother, Diane, knew from the time her son Jacob was two years old that something was not right. Jacob's out-of-control behavior prevented Diane and her husband, Eric, from both attending a home fellowship group offered by their church. When they left him in the church nursery so they could attend a worship service, they usually received parenting advice from the pre-school teacher when they picked Jacob up.

Their feelings that Jacob had a disability of some sort were confirmed when he was disenrolled (the polite term for getting "kicked out," says Diane—as you might be "let go" instead of "fired") from three preschools. When upset, Jacob would kick, hit, throw things, and knock over desks so that he had to be re-strained. At that point, he resorted to head-butting the teacher. No discipline that had succeeded with their older child, Emily, worked with Jacob.

Eventually a pediatrician and child psychiatrist diagnosed Jacob with attention deficit hyperactivity disorder (ADHD) and oppositional defiance disorder (ODD). Diane and Eric were relieved to have professionals identify the source of his diffi-culties, and this has led to treatment options resulting in a happier, better-controlled child.

With the application of a diagnosis, options open up to help the family deal with behavioral differences, providing a better sense of control over the issue.

Public school districts usually offer free testing. Birth-to-three programs or special education preschools can be espe-cially helpful to a child.

When a child is assessed for special education, he's given an IEP (Individualized Education Plan) that can help him qualify for many different kinds of services, including tutoring. Diane described her son Jacob's IEP as "a godsend."

Another big breakthrough for Jacob came when his school principal said, "We've *got* to find a way to make him successful." He was put in a special education pullout class for kids in kindergarten through second grade, which initially met half days only and required Jacob to make fewer transitions during the day.

Jacob was also prescribed medication to help him control his behavior. While effective, it suppressed his appetite. Diane, a registered dietitian and certified diabetes educator, knew the importance of his eating enough to keep his emotions stable and prevent excessive weight loss. She often uses creative means (such as protein shakes) to coerce her strong-willed child to eat so his body can grow and his emotions can stabilize.

Diane has found that when she's offered parenting tips that simply don't work with Jacob, it's best for her to say, "That's very good advice, but this is not a parenting issue. Other things are going on with our child, and we have to take a special approach with him because his needs are different." This opens doors to increased support, instead of shutting them.

IF YOUR CHILD IS DISABLED

Support systems open up when differences are properly identified—and the source of help can be a child's peers, the parents' friends and family, or strangers and organizations.

Books, articles, mail lists, and Web sites also may offer tools to help parents nurture, teach, and appreciate their child more or to offer hope and inspiration for the future.

Some help is from parents who have "been there, done that."

In addition, the Internet is now a useful tool. Mail lists (e-mails that whole groups can contribute to) help members encourage each other on an ongoing basis. You may even start a message board or Web site offering some of the helpful resources you uncover. Of course no one else's child is identical to yours, but you can share practical ideas.

The way to find such lists, books, articles, or Web sites on-line is by *using the key words and the very labels you may hate to use.* Even if you would not call your child ADHD but know that he has some trouble focusing and is highly energetic, an Internet site or book that offers tips to parents whose kids have been diagnosed as ADHD may be helpful.

Key words like *defiant* or SWC (short for *strong-willed child)* may help you find resources for disciplining. Even if you never call your child "stubborn" out loud (the flip side of "determined"), you may realize that *is* a strong component of your child's personality and that you need help! Searching the Web may lead you to new ideas, such as offering your strong-willed child choices instead of threats, which can lead to more harmony and cooperation in your home.

It's important to remember that even with patient, informed, loving guidance, a child with differences may struggle for years. There may be no quick fix. Still, diagnosing a disability can lead to increased understanding at school and in the home—sometimes even resulting in increased affection between that child and a parent or siblings.

After Jacob was diagnosed, Diane's husband, Eric, attended sessions with Jacob's child psychiatrist. When Eric was laid off from work, he also spent more time at home with Jacob. For about a year, while Diane worked and Eric hunted for a job, Eric was Jacob's primary caregiver and got involved in his son's classroom.

Meanwhile, Diane saw a huge attitude shift in her husband. As Eric saw his child's special needs—not just his misbehavior—the two went from frequent conflict to playful affection. The family dynamics changed as both parents realized how negative consequences simply did not work with their child, but reward systems did. And as they better understood Jacob's disability, they also could see their son's gifts: at age three Jacob could draw 3-D objects and use blocks to build incredible structures—not just houses but whole towns with roads. He exhibits fascinating mechanical reasoning and logic. Diane and Eric find ways to encourage Jacob's expression of things he does well.

One of the most critical things you can give your child is a sense of self-worth. It may help to remember that in a dozen years of schooling, your child will have almost fifty different teachers. You will be the only constant! By exploring your child's strengths and ensuring that teachers know what those are, you can boost your child's self-esteem enormously. And with the help of Jesus Christ, you can help your child see his worth as an individual.

7

LOVE IS A VERB

Good parenting is about how you handle the moments.
It's about consistently using the moments well.
This is where we all fall down, but with God's help
(which we should be asking for daily) we can get better at it.

RICK OSBORNE, *PARENTING AT THE SPEED OF LIFE*[1]

When I first walked into the Murfitt home, I saw a one-dimensional picture: a family with a young teen whose disabilities are immediately and painfully obvious.

Fourteen-year-old Gabe, whom I introduced in chapter 3, is only about three feet high. In each of Gabe's legs, his femur is fused together with his tibia and fibula at an angle that results in his knees looking permanently crossed.[2] His arms are only about two inches long, so he can't reach above or behind him and most of his fingers don't work the way they should. He also uses a hearing aid. To get around, Gabe uses an electric wheelchair or rocks on his bottom and knees.

My first thoughts were about how the family copes with his

physical disability, especially in light of my former work in occupational therapy. I know that caring for a disabled child can be worrisome and exhausting.

Yet within a few minutes, I began to see the picture a little more clearly. I saw what the local newspaper reporters and the crews from *Oprah* and *Good Morning America* saw: an amazingly determined kid in an incredibly loving and supportive family.

Gabe's family continually encourages him to "go for it," whatever "it" is, from playing basketball to going to junior high dances. They have confidence in him and are willing to let him try anything he thinks he might be able to do. For example, when in elementary school, Gabe asked his mom if he could help her reconcile her credit card statements on the computer. For three years now he's done it with one-finger typing. Recently the Murfitts hiked up Mount Rainier with friends, everyone taking turns carrying Gabe in a special backpack they had made for him.

As I sat longer with Gabe; his mother, Gigi; his father, Steve; and his seventeen-year-old brother, Zane, the secret for their appeal became clearer. It's not the media attention they've drawn or even Gabe's incredible accomplishments. Instead, it is their absolute delight in one another and faith that God will work even in their difficult situation.

It's clear that Gigi and Steve treasure *both* their children. This first became obvious when I asked Gigi and Steve what they most appreciated about their family. Steve said, "I admire Gabe's courage and his ability to improvise. When Gabe can't do things in the same way as other people, he simply figures out how to get it done." As a baby, Gabe figured out on his own how to hold a bottle to his mouth using his feet.

Gigi added, "A lot of people are drawn to Gabe. He's a leader in his school, and more mature than other kids." As we chatted, out of the corner of my eye I saw Gabe gently, deliberately tumble over the side of his armchair and onto the back of his dog to give his pet a snuggle. He grinned at me.

Gigi and Steve also have much to say about their seventeen-year-old son, Zane, who is part of a musical group called Generation X that does assemblies for schools. He's passionate about Bible study too. Zane is intuitive about painful situations other people might be going through. Perhaps he was given this gift to help his parents cope with the shock of Gabe's severe limb deficiencies, as well as to help others outside his family.

What can we, even those of us whose kids don't have physical struggles, learn from Gabe and his family about treasuring our own children? Here are some ideas:

Remember that your appreciation of your child helps shape his—and your—image of God. Zane told me his parents have greatly influenced his impression of who God is and what it is to have a relationship with Christ.

When Gabe was born, Steve, a former athlete, was bitter and angry. He mostly focused on what Gabe would never be able to accomplish. Steve told me that later that, when he turned to Christ and began giving his worries to Him, he felt more peace and relief that he was not going it alone. "I realized that Someone bigger was in control," he said. As his faith has grown, he's looked more at what Gabe *can* do instead of what he can't do and is proud of his son. The more he encourages Zane and Gabe, the more they see their Father God, not just their father, Steve.

Gigi's love for God is apparent—in fact, she radiates it. And she looks so lovingly at her sons that it must make it easy for them to imagine the twinkle in God's eyes as He looks upon them.

Remember that your kids may teach you something very important. Gabe and Zane are spiritual models for their parents as well. When a trip to Chicago for Gabe to be interviewed on *The Oprah Winfrey Show* was initially postponed (it was later rescheduled), Steve was especially disappointed because the family had been offered tickets to a Cubs game. But he felt humbled when his son Zane gently asked him, "Dad, why are we doing this? Isn't it to encourage kids with disabilities to try more things through seeing what Gabe does? Isn't it to get teachers to give kids more opportunities?"

Remember that God may use your child's difficulties as a platform from which to encourage others. After Gabe threw out the first pitch at a Seattle Mariners baseball game, he received a standing ovation. That's because we all need to see people who make us believe almost anything is possible with enough determination.

But life at the Murfitts' is not always easy. The family does struggle with Gabe's limitations, as he needs help with some of his basic needs. Gabe accepts his abilities, but of course he would love to be healed. He can only imagine what it would be like to unfold his legs and run like other teens. Yet Gabe and his family realize that as more people hear about how they cope and—even better—experience hope, they have opportunities to encourage others. People can see they are not just overcomers but people of faith—a faith everyone could use.

Remember that treasuring your child is a legacy he or she will pass down not only to siblings but also to the next generation. When I asked Gigi whether she felt appreciated as a child, she said that her mother, a single parent and mother of ten kids, had somehow made Gigi feel "the most special." Do you find yourself encouraging your kids in ways your parents encouraged you? Also, do you see your kids encouraging each other as Zane does Gabe?

Remember to encourage your kids through praise, Scripture promises, and motivational phrases. Gigi often tells her kids, "You are so amazing!"

She also shows them encouraging Scripture verses. One day Gabe told his mother that Philippians 4:13, which is framed in their bathroom, is his favorite verse. And so appropriate it is: "I can do all things through Christ who strengthens me" (NKJV).

At some point the Murfitts realized that Scripture reference corresponded with Gabe's birthday: April 13–4/13. Gabe was born on a Good Friday, two days before Easter. Gigi told me that even though she despaired when she first saw her son after his birth—in a sense, her dream of having a perfectly healthy child died that Friday—hope was resurrected within her heart by that Easter Sunday.

No matter what Gabe does, he can count on God to give him strength: whether that means bravely getting out on a basketball court or being willing to humble himself enough to let his friends carry him up a mountain. And fourteen years later, he

with yours and to help you remember the positive side of those characteristics.

· to help you accept what you cannot change in your child and to grant you wisdom to know how to bring about change in the areas you can.

Way #2: Show Joy When You See Him

Stop, look, and listen to your child as often as you can: "light up" (a term from Gary Smalley) when you see him. The look on your face is the first thing that will persuade your child you love him.

In an old television commercial, a man and woman joyfully run toward each other across a field in slow motion with arms outstretched, their clothes and hair blowing gently in the wind. I've felt time slow a little like that over the years while watching my kids stampede to the door, crying out "Daddy, Daddy, Daddy!" or bounce down the stairs to be first to get to the door when a friend arrives. When they see someone special coming, they don't just call out casually from the other room, "Just come on in." They don't look up briefly from paperwork or the TV and mumble, "Oh . . . hi." Instead, each time they treat the arrival like a magnificent homecoming, worthy of a full investment of mind, body, and emotion.

WHEN WAS THE LAST TIME YOUR FACE LIT UP WHEN YOUR CHILD ENTERED THE ROOM?

When was the last time your face lit up when your child entered the room? When did you last welcome her home with a sweeping hug? Make it a goal to smile broadly and perhaps even rush to embrace your child when she comes home from school or from a playdate.

Also, outlaw some facial expressions. No eye-rolling. No glaring. No lack of eye contact. That doesn't mean you must be happy, happy, happy all the time. (There's a children's gospel song suggesting that, which I find very annoying.) It simply means you will not permit looks on your face that might appear sarcastic, hostile, or indifferent. Open up your face, hold your gaze a little longer than usual, and smile broadly. When your child smiles back, you'll discover it is infectious.

Sounds simple, doesn't it? But the demands and pace of life can make really delighting in our kids tough to do consistently. You may need to leave yourself notes in a few places that say something like "Light up!" or "My child is: [write down some words from the Temperament ABCs]." Try placing Post-it notes inside the kitchen cupboards or on cereal boxes—anywhere you might surprise yourself and be reminded to do an attitude check. (If your child sees the notes, so much the better!)

When you deliberately choose a new attitude toward your child, new actions will begin to flow from that. They may not be the most creative in the world, but believe me, your child will not care. A good old-fashioned bear hug can be just as powerful as a cutesy little sandwich with the words "You're special" written on it.

Way #3: Recognize—and Rejoice in—Your Child's Giftedness

All children have gifts of one kind or another. Sometimes, as when a child is gifted in academics, music, sports, or art, the abilities are obvious to everyone. When a child strongly possesses an attribute like generosity, others may overlook it. Yet that can be a tremendous gift to others and may even point to a spiritual gift: a way that God will use a person throughout her lifetime to reach others for Him.

My son, Tyler, has intellectual abilities that were evident from the time he was very young, as were Elisa's agility and athleticism. And since Aimee was tiny, we've seen her unique ability to connect with people sensitively and compassionately.

Do you know what makes your child remarkable? Sometimes in the day-to-day drudgery of living, we cannot see or do not appreciate our child's abilities. Yet doing so will enrich life for you both. That's why I invite you to take a few minutes to complete the "Strengths Test." No, it is not a scientific survey; however, you know your child better than anyone else, so the raw data is already in your head. And, by the way, there's no penalty for "cheating": Feel free to get your child's take on the questions as well.

If difficulties with your child make it impossible for you to list any strengths right now, I encourage you to make this a matter of prayer and perhaps even to talk to someone like your child's teacher or school counselor who can help you see him more objectively. Does your child make others laugh? Is she polite? Is he a mechanical whiz?

After you've completed the test, take a few moments to revel in your child's strengths. Can you identify with the psalmist who wrote: "Your works are wonderful, I know that full well" (Psalm 139:14)?

STRENGTHS TEST

PHYSICAL ABILITIES
Coordinated
Rhythmic
Strong
Flexible

MENTAL ABILITIES
Organized thinker
Problem solver
Good memorizer
Linguistic
Numerical

CREATIVE ABILITIES
Artistic
Crafty
Dramatic
Musical
A writer

INTERACTING ABILITIES
Witty
Sociable
Mediator
Leader
Empathizer

1. What activity causes my child to shine with energy and passion?

_____

_____

_____

2. For what do other adults (and children) compliment my child?

_____

_____

_____

3. What would my child do if he or she had a free afternoon?

_____

_____

_____

4. What makes my child unique from other kids?

_____

_____

_____

5. Have his teachers identified an area of strength?

_____

_____

_____

6. To what kinds of toys or supplies does my child gravitate?

_____

_____

_____

7. Whom does my child admire? Who are her heroes?

_____

_____

_____

8. When I watch my child interact with others, the character quality that I most appreciate is . . .

_____

_____

_____

9. When he grows up I can picture my child being a . . .

_____

_____

_____

10. My child can do this better than anyone I know:

_____

_____

_____

Way #4: Admire Your Child's Strengths without Going Overboard

Now comes the challenge: How do we nurture our child's strengths without praising the wrong things?

DO . . . acknowledge your child's gifts without overemphasizing or underemphasizing them. When you consider your child's gifts, avoid the two extremes. On the one hand, be careful not to attach too much significance to your child's abilities. No matter what gifts a child possesses, exaggerated feelings of pride will not be valued by others or by God, who loves all children equally. Some parents of children who've been labeled academically gifted, for instance, must learn to deal with their own pride, resisting the temptation to show off their child's abilities. It's a very real temptation, and I've had to avoid that urge myself. (If you see signs that your child may be intellectually gifted, see appendix B, "Special Challenges of the Specially Gifted." While most people would assume giftedness must bring unmitigated delight, it can bring its own challenges to the parent-child relationship.)

Don't make the mistake of minimizing your child's gifts either. Some parents do this because they fear their child might develop a prideful spirit. If a child is never praised for what he does well, however, he may think he can never be good enough to please Mom or Dad—or perhaps even God. In addition, he may miss out on the joy of living out the purpose for which he was created.

DO . . . let your child take the lead in how much effort she wants to expend developing her gifts. Parents of highly capable kids are often eyed suspiciously and accused of pushing their children. It's true that some zealous parents use flash cards with toddlers to teach early reading and some of those children may learn to read early, but that doesn't necessarily mean they are gifted. Conversely, intellectually gifted children don't always read early. Some are dyslexic or simply lack the inclination to read, choosing to focus energies elsewhere.

Yet intellectually advanced children, instead of being pushed, tend to pull their parents. They initiate learning, pestering their parents to teach them in their areas of interest. A gifted toddler who is fascinated with the alphabet may search eagerly for letters on road signs, license plates, or cereal boxes. He may teach himself to write at the same time he's learning how to hold a fat crayon.

DO . . . remember that you set the limits. Although you may take many cues from your kids, as the parent you often are the best judge of how much to encourage your child to work at a certain area. Sometimes a parent is fully aware of a child's natural gifts, yet unwilling to succumb to pressures to get the kid into related elite or expensive programs.

> BE CAREFUL NOT TO ATTACH TOO MUCH SIGNIFICANCE TO YOUR CHILD'S ABILITIES—BUT DON'T MAKE THE MISTAKE OF MINIMIZING YOUR CHILD'S GIFTS EITHER.

I wish I had a dollar for every time someone has seen Elisa jump, flip, or climb and said, "You *should* sign her up for [XYZ athletic program]." Some have even implied that I'm wasting her talent (although no one yet has offered to fork over the cash for her to train for the Olympic Games).

This past summer we finally enrolled her in her first formal class. Not surprisingly, her coaches immediately picked up on her abilities. As they encourage us to consider further training, we must consider several questions: How much time will involvement in Elisa's athletic program steal from family dinners? Will competitions conflict with church times or other family activities? Can we afford it financially? What injuries are common in this sport, and how can those be avoided? Is it worth getting a child started early, on the slim hope that she might earn scholarships or compete in that sport?

We also must consider Elisa's well-being. Does she love gymnastics enough to dedicate so much time to it? Will it steal time that she could use to explore other interests? These are questions only a parent will ask in depth. So even as we delight in Elisa's gifts, we realize that sometimes the most loving thing we can do is set limits.

DO . . . remind your child to be thankful for his gifts. Help your child remember that God has given him those gifts that you praise. Talk with your child about why God might have given him his gifts and how he might use them to help draw other people to Him or change the world somehow.

DO . . . let your child know it is okay to fail. Remind her that failure can be a big part of learning. Remember that you can praise efforts as well as results.

One fifth grader, who is used to excelling in the classroom, may be despondent about getting a B+ on a report card full of A's. A classmate who is a standout on his soccer team may berate himself for not making that goal.

However, if a child is always taught to avoid failure, he may never take risks or embrace failure as one path to learning.

Don't assume that just because a child is talented, his self-image is healthy.

DO . . . make your love unconditional. To boost their child's self-esteem, some parents constantly praise their child's performance. This can make it seem like their love is conditional—that a child is loved only for her special abilities.

When a child who usually gets straight A's brings home a C, perhaps that might be a time not just to encourage him to do his best but also to reassure him that you love him no matter what.

Christian singer and songwriter Michael Card, who has a number of awards and best-selling CDs to his credit, often remarks, "You are not your gift."[4] That's a great reminder of the importance of making our kids realize that we (and God) love them for who they are, not for what they do. Furthermore, we love them because of who they are today, not because of what they might be someday.

Way #5: Use Words Creatively

For some kids, words of affirmation are especially important. Aimee even put a mailbox on her door in hopes of receiving "mail" from family members!

I, too, am a word person and my desire for sentimental words appears to be a bit of a joke in my home. For some recent event, considering our lean budget, I said all I really wanted was a mushy card. I opened a package from Gordy to find a squishy ball on which he'd drawn a playing card and the words "Mushy Card." I almost threw the ball at him but laughed because it showed that he does hear me.

Here are some creative ways you can use words to express affection to your child:

- Try to incorporate your child's attributes into compliments about concrete things he or she does. "That was resourceful of you to set up your own lemonade stand. You have some good ideas!"
- When you have more time, consider making lists of attributes in an acrostic of her name on a handmade card.
- A candy poster is especially fun—write a message with candy bars taped where some words would be, like "I have GOOD AND PLENTY of fun with you!"
- Consider making your computer screen saver a scrolling message like "I love my kids." It will delight your kids and remind you to express your affection to them.
- Make up funny word games or songs incorporating your child's name. You can make up a tune or borrow another familiar one and add your own words off the cuff.

When Tyler was a baby I sang to the tune of "Bingo": "There was a mom who had a boy and Tyler was his name-oh, T-Y-L-E-R . . ." I made up Aimee's song when as a toddler she was constantly exploring: "Whatcha doing, Aimee-waimie, whatcha doing, what's your game . . . how I love my Aimee-waimie. . ." Elisa's was to the tune of "La Cucaracha": "Oh, oh Elisa, hu hu Katrina, oh, you are my little girl. . . ."

None of these will make the Top Ten. But they were fun and for some silly reason they stuck—in fact, my kids still remember them.

Way #6: Keep in Touch

While Aimee loves words of affirmation, Elisa warms to touch. When I asked her how often a parent should hug a child, she said. "Once before breakfast, another before lunch, another after lunch . . ." (Are hugs food for the skin and emotions?)

Consider using one or more of these ideas to use touch to express your love:

- Silly kisses and hugs are great.
- "Eat" one of your child's ears while saying how delicious it is: "Mmmm, it tastes just like chocolate!" Then nibble on her other ear and say, "Ick! This one tastes like spinach! No, wait, yum . . . now it tastes like gumdrops!" Keep alternating ears as your child giggles.
- Draw alphabet letters on your child's back and ask him to guess which letter you've made.
- At bedtime, stroke your child's hair gently away from her face as she is nodding off and you are praying for her. (Aimee calls these "face rubbies.")
- Be a tickle-monster.
- Do lots of story snuggles.
- Dance!

As boys grow older, they tend to prefer a casual arm punch, a high five, or a quick wrestle with Dad instead of snuggling. But a boy with sports-related aches and pains will rarely turn down a shoulder massage from Mom, if she puts some real muscle into it. And even when good-bye hugs in front of peers become no-no's, a quick peck on the cheek—no buddies around—is usually A-OK.

Way #7: Give Gifts of Appreciation

Give simple tokens of appreciation. Our friend Lester playfully gave Elisa an old key attached to an unexciting key ring with a business logo on it, telling her it was the key to his heart. You would think that it's a golden key, the way she's worried a few times when she's misplaced it. I think the greatest significance of that object is that it offers her a tangible reminder that she's valuable enough to be offered the key to someone's heart. I wish I'd thought of giving her a key first!

As Elisa proved, even an old key can take on significance for a child. When presenting your child a simple object, attach some significance to it. For example:

- Present him with a gift he has worked for. This may sound like an oxymoron, but it's not. Letting your child strive to earn something he really wants can be very exciting to him. A toy earned as a result of hard work can be more thrilling than one given at his first request.
- Occasionally buy foods you usually say no to. If you generally turn down your child's request for an expensive junk cereal because of its cost and lack of nutrition, someday bring a box home as a surprise.
- Provide the gift of an allowance and a clothes budget. I've seen firsthand how excited Aimee is when she finds a shirt she loves at a bargain price that fits within her budget. I've seen as well the ho-hum response of a friend of hers who

can buy whatever she wants but confesses that she always feels unsatisfied.

Way #8: Turn Attitudes into Actions

Take a look at the "Actions of Appreciation" sidebar. Make it a point to reveal your love through as many of the ways listed as possible, every day. You might post this "report card" on your refrigerator as a reminder!

MOST OF THE ACTIONS THAT WILL SHOW LOVE TO YOUR CHILD ARE NOT EARTHSHAKING—BUT MANY SMALL ACTIONS WILL REVEAL A LOVING ATTITUDE.

Create family rituals and celebrations, especially for birthdays, to really make your child feel special. We follow a birthday routine for everyone in our family: We begin by entering the birthday person's room (while it's still dark) with a burning candle stuck in a piece of toast or a pancake, singing "Happy Birthday." Before dinner, we set the table with our official birthday tablecloth—most often with our good china and wine glasses for sparkling cider. The birthday child requests the dinner menu and often wears a silly birthday beanie. The blessing includes thanks for that child's presence in our lives. Later we watch at least part of a home movie of that child when he or she was younger.

Most of the actions that will show love to your child are not earthshaking—but many small actions will reveal a loving attitude. To some kids, seeing your love in action—from helping them find lost objects to making sure a favorite shirt is washed—is most meaningful. I can be lazy and expect that a love note will make my child feel good because words are *my*

ACTIONS OF APPRECIATION

Your Daily Report Card

Our kids get report cards to keep them motivated. Why not us? Rate yourself on how well you affirm your child using the criteria in bold. (See the list that follows each for examples.) Start fresh every day!

S+ (Super: You truly enjoy your child, don't you?)
S (Satisfactory: You communicate well to your child your love and acceptance.)
N (Needs Work: How can you help your child feel more appreciated?)
Note: Expect a mix of S+'s, S's and N's: Straight S's would be a miraculous achievement.

TIME FOR BED! FOR TODAY ONLY, RATE YOUR:

S+	S	N	
			BODY LANGUAGE: smiles, frequent eye contact, gentle tickles or "face rubbies", hugs, eyes lighting up

S+	S	N	
			CONVERSATION: gentle tone of voice, sense of humor without resorting to sarcasm, more praises than correction, correcting, not obsessing or nagging, concrete instead of vague directions, discussing your child's interests and longings, sharing God's promises

S+	S	N	
			ANTICIPATION OF NEEDS: food and clothing, safety, medical, dental, eye care, school needs, social needs, development of your child's gifts and interests, R & R

S+	S	N	
			AVAILABILITY: for scraped knees, kids' concerts, sports, etc., kids' emotional crises, teaching life skills, parent-child play

S+	S	N

BALANCE OF FREEDOM WITH BOUNDARIES: firm when necessary, offer choices, protect your child, trust your child, let your child learn from mistakes

S+	S	N

FORGIVENESS: fresh every morning, communicated to your child

S+	S	N

ENCOURAGEMENT OF FAMILY BONDING VIA: family meals, activities or vacations, siblings attending each other's events, keeping extended family connected and in tune with your child's growth and dreams

Do you have days where you feel you've earned all N's? All parents do! But it's likely you underestimate your impact; your child might give you raving S+'s.

Circle what you do well and ask God to help you with the rest, remembering—as Scarlett O'Hara said—"Tomorrow is another day."

thing, when a particular child won't read my note because she's feeling offended that too often I've said I'd help her "later" and later never comes.

Since I'm big on independence and responsibility, I expect my kids to do things on their own as much as possible, but I try to remember the impact of an unexpected favorite breakfast, cheerfully running them on an errand, or even a surprise bailout (taking a forgotten school paper to a child when he knows you'd normally let him suffer the consequences).

As for basic care of your child, don't underestimate how much your child appreciates that. When I asked Elisa how good parents reveal their love for their kids, she startled me by saying, "By making sure they get shots so they don't get sicknesses and making them brush their teeth so they don't get cavities." What do you know!

Way #9: Spend Time Together
• Play
• Play
• Play

No matter what, you and your child both benefit from time together, which is why I'm so big on play. As you and your child laugh and learn together, you'll discover that a playdate can be words, touch, and an act of service all rolled into one. Once you are actually doing something—anything—with your child, the moment often snowballs into something bigger than you expected, even when you've agreed grudgingly to spend "just a few minutes together."

One day I'd promised to play Candy Land with my daughter, which frankly didn't thrill me. I tried to focus not on the game but on time with her, but when she wanted to go a second time around the board, the "board-um" was more than I could bear.

"But we just got started!" she said indignantly when I tried to quit. "That wasn't any time together at all!"

Hmm. How could I make that time more fun? I took a second look at the colored cards and mysteriously began sorting them into piles of two. Then I said, "Let's play Go-Fish with them! A pair of Queen Frostines will get you fifteen points; double purples, ten; and single oranges, five."

We got the giggles asking, "Do you have a Plumpy?" and exclaiming, "I got a pair of Grandma Nuts!" and drew a second child into the fun. We added an extra rule for good measure. Now we had to yell out a warning if we only had one card left in our hand . . . and Candy-Fish UNO was born.

Time for love also includes attending your child's sports events, honor assemblies, science fairs, or concerts. Be prepared to take lots of pictures and clap wildly when appropriate!

At our local high school's homecoming game last fall, I got a lump in my throat at the sight of Donna and Imani cheering for Cameron, one of the players. They were wearing school colors, wildly waving pom-poms, and screaming, "Go, Cameron, go!!!" For so many years there'd been an empty spot on the bleachers where Cameron's family should have been.

It doesn't hurt to ask your child which events are most important to him. My son told us he honestly didn't care if we went to out-of-town wrestling matches (Whew!) but made it clear he wanted to see our faces in the bleachers when he had meets at home. I tried to learn what I could about the sport to generate more enthusiasm and know when to "Yay!" and when to murmur "Awwww."

Elisa's one-sentence solo at the first grade concert was not to be missed—meaning I had to say no to a free ticket to the Fifth Avenue "the-a-tah" the same night (sigh). But the choice for me was a no-brainer. My child was counting on me. And she would only have one first-grade musical.

Your child will appreciate not only special events but the times when you schedule dates together to do nothing in particular. Setting a time and place—even if it's just "two o'clock this afternoon for half an hour"—and labeling it a date "for just you and me and *nobody* else!" doesn't mean you need to do anything particularly special, as long as you're together.

After all, it is the small moments that add up to the days, weeks, months, and years of your child's life. Make the most of every one you can.

DELIGHTING IN TODAY

Author and speaker Becky Freeman once said, "Children give depth to our lives: Like those magic pictures that seem one-dimensional, until you move in closer, cross your eyes, and discover there's more there than you ever imagined."[5]

I have trouble getting my eyes to cooperate when I try to see the hidden image within one of those two-dimensional pictures. I've been told that to actually see the hidden picture, you must look at it while relaxing your eyes.

By the same token, sometimes we simply need to look more purposefully at our children and relax more when we are with them, which will increase our awareness of their complexity and hidden talents. It may take years to get to know your child in depth. Listen intently. Look deliberately and with expectation. Eventually you will get beyond the superficial. As hidden attributes in your child begin to emerge before your eyes, you will experience surprise, awe, and delight.

What about right now? No matter what time or family pressures you face, no matter how much you struggle to understand and live peacefully with a difficult child, don't miss out on the joy you can reap *today.*

It's time . . . to put down this book, walk into the other room, and tell your child what you love about him or her. Enjoy the hugs and kisses that will be your reward.

is living up to his favorite saying: "Attitude, not aptitude, determines your altitude!"[3]

What about you? Do you find yourself encouraging your kids, even when they wear you out? Do you see your kids already doing the same for their siblings? Every time I hear my kids enthusiastically tell each other "Good job!" I feel that perhaps I'm doing my own job right.

NINE MORE WAYS TO TREASURE YOUR KIDS

When it comes to expressing love to our kids, it's not necessarily the creativity of activities but your attitude and the consistency in connecting with your child that are so critical. No matter how you express "I love you" to your children, it doesn't mean much unless it reassures them that you really do.

ASK GOD TO HELP YOU ACCEPT WHAT YOU CANNOT CHANGE IN YOUR CHILD AND TO GRANT YOU WISDOM TO KNOW HOW TO BRING ABOUT CHANGE IN THE AREAS YOU CAN.

You can cultivate an attitude of appreciation. With that attitude, the simplest expressions can be very powerful.

Way #1: Talk to God about Your Child
When you wake up tomorrow, immediately thank God for your child.

If you anticipate struggles that day because of your child's personality or a certain situation you're facing, ask God

• to help you see your child's positive traits in the situation.
• to give you patience to deal with those traits that conflict

NOTES

Chapter 1: Delighted or Disillusioned?

[1] *Webster's Third New International Dictionary,* s.v. "delight."

[2] Judith Viorst, *Alexander and the Terrible, Horrible, No Good, Very Bad Day* (New York: Macmillan Publishing Company, 1972).

[3] See Matthew 18:12-14.

[4] See Mark 10:13-16 and Matthew 18:2-4.

[5] See Neil Baldwin, *Edison: Inventing the Century* (New York: Hyperion, 1995), 20; the January 1 entry in *God's Little Devotional Journal for Moms* (Colorado Springs: Honor Books, 2001); and Richard Lingeman, *Small Town America: A Narrative History, 1620–the Present* (New York: GP Putnam's Sons, 1980).

[6] Arthur J. Palmer, "So Rich a Life," a forty-page typescript (memoir) quoted by Neil Baldwin in *Edison: Inventing the Century* (New York: Hyperion, 1995), 18. (Italics appeared in this work.)

[7] Jennifer Edwards, "Report Cited Summit Risk," *Cincinnati Enquirer* (January 22, 2004).

Chapter 2: Tough Stuff

[1] Max Lucado, *A Gentle Thunder: Hearing God through the Storm* (Nashville: W Publishing Group, 2001), 122.

[2] Richard Scuderi, MD, PhD, Medical Editorial Board, http://www.sleep-deprivation.com.

[3] American College of Obstetricians and Gynecologists, "Answers to Common Questions about Postpartum Depression," http://www.acog.org/from_home/publications/press_releases/nr01-08-02.cfm.

[4] Sheila Walsh, *The Heartache No One Sees* (Nashville: Thomas Nelson, 2004), 58.

[5] One such organization is Ramah International, a nonprofit ministry designed to assist those hurting from postabortion syndrome by providing resources and referrals to local postabortion ministry programs. See http://www.ramahinternational.org.

[6] Barbour Publishing has released several versions of *The Bible Promise Book* for women, teens, graduates, and others. Verses are categorized by key words (anxiety, fear, depression, etc.). Tyndale House Publishers has released a simi-

lar line called *Touchpoints,* which includes verses for different situations. These inexpensive paperbacks are wonderful to keep on hand to give to someone who is hurting or to use yourself when you're feeling down.

Chapter 3: From DNA to Birth Day

[1] Robert P. George, *The Clash of Orthodoxies* (Wilmington, Del.: ISI Books, 2001), 320.

[2] *A Bug's Life,* Walt Disney Pictures/Pixar studios, 1998; original story by John Lasseter, Andrew Stanton, and Joe Ranft; directed by Lasseter and Stanton.

[3] See http://www.forensic-evidence.com.

[4] Barry Werth and Alexander Tsiaras, *From Conception to Birth: A Life Unfolds* (New York: Doubleday, 2002), 5.

[5] Paul Brand and Philip Yancey, *Fearfully and Wonderfully Made* (Grand Rapids: Zondervan, 1980), 28, 45.

[6] Lori B. Andrews, "Designer Babies," *Reader's Digest* 158 (July 2001): 68; and Gladys Pollack, *Reader's Digest Canada,* www.readersdigest.ca/mag/2001.

[7] Larry Burkett and Rick Osborne, *Your Child Wonderfully Made* (Chicago: Moody Publishers, 1998), 23.

[8] Janet L. Hopson, "Fetal Psychology," *Psychology Today* (October 1998). See also http://www.realchoices.com/FetalPsychology.pdf.

[9] Daniel Taylor and Ronald Hoekstra, *Before Their Time: Lessons in Living from Those Born Too Soon* (Downers Grove, Ill.: InterVarsity Press, 2000).

[10] Rosalie Icenhower, *Don't Sing Any Sad Songs: A Down Syndrome Daughter's Joyful Journey* (Frederick, Md.: PublishAmerica, 2000).

[11] *Door to Door,* Warner Home Video, 2002. Based on the true story of Bill Porter and the impact his mother had on his life. Note: Some of the dialogue spoken between fictional characters (composites of Bill's customers as a Watkins product salesman) is inconsistent with biblical principles. Letters from Bill's friends and customers can be read in the book by Shelly Brady, *Ten Things I Learned from Bill Porter* (Novato, Calif.: New World Library, 2002).

Chapter 4: Personality Potluck

[1] References are to personality typing systems developed or written about by Isabel Briggs Meyers, David Keirsey, Florence Littauer, Gary Smalley and John Trent, and Tim LaHaye.

[2] John Trent et al., *The Treasure Tree: Helping Kids Understand Their Personality* (Nashville: Thomas Nelson, 1998).

Chapter 5: Clash and Burn

[1] Ian Falconer, *Olivia* (New York: Simon & Schuster, 2002).

[2] For more information on this remarkable woman, see http://www.sharirusch.com.

[3] Mel Levine, *A Mind at a Time* (New York: Simon & Schuster, 2002), 37.

[4] Stella Chess and Alexander Thomas, *Know Your Child: An Authoritative Guide for Today's Parents* (New York: Basic Books, 1987).

[5] Levine, *A Mind at a Time,* 23.

[6] For more insights into helping children who dread school, see Cynthia Tobias, *I Hate School: How to Help Your Child Love Learning* (Grand Rapids, Mich.: Zondervan, 2004).

[7] Susan M. Miller, *Reading Too Soon: How to Understand and Help the Hyperlexic Child* (Chicago: Center for Speech & Language, 1993), 5.

Chapter 6: Disability Dilemmas

[1] Levine, *A Mind at a Time,* 46.

[2] In this chapter, the names of the children with disabilities as well as those of their family members and friends have been changed to protect their privacy.

[3] Figures obtained from the National Institute of Mental Health Web site. See http://www.nimh.nih.gov/publicat/adhd.cfm#intro.

[4] Demitri F. Papolos and Janice Papolos, *The Bipolar Child: The Definitive and Reassuring Guide to Childhood's Most Misunderstood Disorder* (New York: Broadway Books, 1999), 218.

[5] For more information on preventing or curbing sibling rivalry, see Adele Faber and Elaine Mazlish, *Siblings without Rivalry* (New York: Perennial Currents, 1998).

Chapter 7: Love Is a Verb

[1] Rick Osborne, *Parenting at the Speed of Life: 60 Ways to Capture Time with Your Kids* (Wheaton, Ill.: Tyndale House, 2004), 124.

[2] Gabe's disability is called pseudothalidomide tetraphocomelia, which in lay terms means "something looking like thalidomide has affected four limbs." One helpful resource for families with limb deficiencies is the Limb Deficiency Clinic at Children's Hospital in Seattle.

[3] This quote has been attributed to both Zig Ziglar and Jesse Jackson.

[4] Sara Groves mentions the influence of Card's statement on her in an online interview at http://womanstouch.ag.org/womanstouch/profiles/sara-

groves.cfm. She also explains how her mom nurtured her gifts as she was growing up.

[5] Becky Freeman, *Peanut Butter Kisses and Mud Pie Hugs* (Eugene, Ore.: Harvest House, 2000), 12.

APPENDIX A

PARENTING RESOURCES

The following resources and organizations are recommended by the author. Inclusion on this list does not necessarily constitute endorsement by Focus on the Family.

RECOMMENDED READING
Helping Your Kids Understand Their Value

Ian Falconer, *Olivia* (New York: Simon & Schuster, 2002).
A picture book about a highly energetic, creative (and sometimes difficult) piglet.

Max Lucado and Sergio Martinez, *You Are Special* (Wheaton, Ill.: Crossway Books, 1997).
A picture book about how a woodcarver, Eli, helps Punchinello, one of his wooden creatures, understand how special he is—no matter what other Wemmicks may think. This book helps children realize that, regardless of how the world sees us, God loves each of us just as we are.

John Trent et al., *The Treasure Tree* (Nashville: Thomas Nelson, 1998).
A picture book that is fun to read with your kids and that will inspire them to think about their personality types. It will also help them learn to appreciate others. Includes a personality straits checklist that you and your child can complete together.

Dealing with Difficult Issues

Julie Ann Barnhill, *She's Gonna Blow! Real Help for Moms Dealing with Anger* (Eugene, Ore.: Harvest House, 2001).

Adele Faber and Elaine Mazlish, *Siblings without Rivalry: How to Help Your Children Live Together, So You Can Live Too* (New York: Avon, 1999).
Practical ideas for diffusing sibling rivalry.

Patricia H. Rushford, *What Kids Need Most in a Mom* (Grand Rapids: Fleming H. Revell, 1999).
A humorous and honest book on how to trust sons and daughters to God's care, instill forgiveness in children, get out of the guilt factory, and share important discoveries with kids.

Daniel Taylor and Ronald Hoekstra, *Before Their Time: Lessons in Living from Those Born Too Soon* (Downers Grove, Ill.: InterVarsity Press, 2000).
Five stories of babies born fifteen to eighteen weeks prematurely. Written from the viewpoint of the Christian physician who worked with the babies and their families.

Coping with Personality and Learning Differences

Pasquale J. Accardo and Barbara Y. Whitman, *Dictionary of Developmental Disabilities Terminology* (Baltimore: Paul H. Brookes Publishing, 1996).
A secular reference book defining terms commonly used to describe disabilities and treatment methods.

Rosalie Icenhower, *Don't Sing Any Sad Songs: A Down Syndrome Daughter's Joyful Journey* (Frederick, Md.: PublishAmerica, 2000).
A biography from the mother of a child with Down Syndrome, written from a Christian perspective.

Carol Stock Kranowitz, *The Out-of-Sync Child: Recognizing and Coping with Sensory Integration Dysfunction* (New York: Perigee Books, 1998).
Parents of children labeled difficult, picky, oversensitive, clumsy, or inattentive may find a new explanation and discover new hope in this book.

This is the first guide for parents on Sensory Integration Dysfunction, written by a preschool teacher with input from occupational therapists and medical doctors. Offers many helpful anecdotal examples and check-lists to help parents determine whether their child struggles in this area.

Carol Stock Kranowitz, *The Out-of-Sync Child Has Fun* (New York: Perigee Books, 2003).
This book features activities that are SAFE: Sensory-motor, Appropriate, Fun, and Easy to help organize a child's brain and body.

Mary Sheedy Kurcinka, *Raising Your Spirited Child* (New York: HarperPerennial, 1992).
A guide for the parent whose child is more intense, sensitive, perceptive, persistent, and energetic. Offers practical suggestions for getting through the day with a "spirited" child.

Mary Sheedy Kurcinka, *Raising Your Spirited Child Workbook* (New York: Perennial Currents, 1998).
A companion workbook to help parents create families where spirit thrives. Techniques to help your child "hear" your message, plans for calming activities, tips for winning your child's cooperation, and ideas for dealing with mealtimes, bedtimes, and meltdowns.

Mel Levine, *A Mind at a Time: America's Top Learning Expert Shows How Every Child Can Succeed* (New York: Simon & Schuster, 2002).
Tales of real children who struggle in school illustrate how attention, memory, language, spatial ordering, sequential ordering, motor skills, higher thinking, and social thinking all affect the way children learn. Levine is a learning disabilities expert and pediatrician.

Susan M. Miller, *Reading Too Soon: How to Understand and Help the Hyperlexic Child* (Chicago: Center for Speech and Language Disorders, 1993).

Dennis Swanberg , Diane Passno, and Walt Larimore, *Why A.D.H.D. Doesn't Mean Disaster* (Wheaton, Ill.: Tyndale House, 2003).

Cynthia Ulrich Tobias, *I Hate School: How to Help Your Child Love Learning* (Grand Rapids, Mich.: Zondervan, 2004).
Don't let a one-size-fits-all educational system steal the joys and riches of learning from your son or daughter. Learning styles expert Cynthia Ulrich Tobias shows how you can work with your child's school and teachers to tailor an education your child will love, not hate.

Cynthia Ulrich Tobias, *The Way They Learn: How to Discover and Teach to Your Child's Strengths* (Wheaton, Ill.: Tyndale House, 1994).

Cynthia Ulrich Tobias, *You Can't Make Me (But I Can Be Persuaded): Strategies for Bringing Out the Best in Your Strong-Willed Child* (Colorado Springs: Waterbrook Press, 1999).

Trying New Attitudes and Actions
Vicki Lansky, *101 Ways to Make Your Child Feel Special* (Chicago: McGraw-Hill, 1991).

Vicki Lansky, *101 Ways to Tell Your Child "I Love You"* (Chicago: McGraw-Hill, 1988).

Kevin Leman, *Bringing Up Your Kids without Tearing Them Down* (Nashville: Thomas Nelson, 1995).

Laurie Winslow Sargent, *The Power of Parent-Child Play* (Wheaton, Ill.: Tyndale House, 2003).
Have fun with your child while teaching values, enhancing confidence, and reducing the need to discipline. Includes ideas on how to overcome barriers to play as well as five-minute-fun activities designed to help you and your child connect.

Council for Exceptional Children (CEC)
Arlington, Virginia
http://www.cec.sped.org
888-CEC-SPED
A professional organization dedicated to improving educational outcomes for gifted students and students with disabilities.

Children and Adults with Attention-Deficit/Hyperactivity Disorder (CHADD)
Landover, Maryland
http://www.chadd.org
800-233-4050
A site designed to help parents of children with ADHD.

Hearts at Home
Normal, Illinios
http://www.hearts-at-home.org
309-888-MOMS
A support organization for moms offering conferences, individual support groups, and other resources, including a magazine.

Moms in Touch, International
Poway, California
http://www.momsintouch.org
800-949-MOMS
Mothers of school-age children meet together to pray for their children's school, their teachers, and the children themselves. E-mail them via their Web site to locate a group near you.

Mothers of Preschoolers (MOPS)

Denver, Colorado

http://www.mops.org

800-929-1287

Mothers of preschoolers meet in local groups to encourage one another, engage in activities, and hear guest speakers on relevant topics. This international organization also produces a magazine and daily two-minute vignettes that air on more than six hundred outlets in the United States and are also available on the Internet.

National Center for Fathering

Kansas City, Missouri

http://www.fathers.com

800-593-DADS

Provides some customized parenting training, as well as speakers on fatherlessness and the impact of a father; also offers small group curriculum and a free quarterly magazine, as well as a weekly e-mail newsletter.

Author's Web Site

http://www.parentchildplay.com

See this site for additional and updated resources, including recommended reading and links, as well as more information about Laurie Winslow Sargent.

APPENDIX B

SPECIAL CHALLENGES OF THE SPECIALLY GIFTED

While every child has gifts and talents, about one in ten will be called intellectually "gifted" by a world that tends to notice and label anyone who stands out in any way. Such kids and their parents face some unique challenges.

FORMAL TESTING

One of the biggest questions for parents of kids who learn "too soon" is whether it's worthwhile to have a child's intelligence formally tested. To some people, that may seem an unnecessary search for a prestigious gifted label for their child. But when the parent of a child comes to an educational crossroads, testing *can* help parents, teachers, and school administrators know what to do with a child.

If you sense your child may be gifted, ask yourself:

- Does she use an advanced vocabulary or like to read books geared for older children?
- Does he learn quickly and easily, recalling important details, concepts, and ideas?
- Does she notice tiny or obscure details?
- Is his curiosity insatiable, or does she get excitement and pleasure from intellectual challenge?
- Can he concentrate for long periods of time?
- Does she understand complex concepts, including mathematical ones?
- Do many things interest him?
- Does she have strong critical thinking skills and tend to be self-critical?

- Is her sense of humor alert and subtle, perhaps evident in her plays on words?
- Does he show creative ability or imaginative expression in areas like music, art, dance, or drama?
- Are her rhythm, movement, and the ways she moves her body unusually controlled?
- Does he show unusual social poise and an ability to communicate with adults in a mature manner?[1]

My sense is that if a child is operating at least two years ahead of his peers in most academic areas and he might be able to participate in a program you know he'd love, it's probably worth testing. If you suspect that your child may be intellectually gifted and need extra challenges, I suggest that you be honest with her. Tell her that testing might give her more options for more interesting classes but not to fret about her performance. Don't call it a gifted education test. Let her know that all kids are gifted in some area, that tests are not perfect ways of measuring intelligence, and that you are not too emotionally invested in the testing.

As you work with your child's teachers to assess her abilities, jot down conversations with your child or observations you make of her abilities. Your notes may come in handy in the future when educational decisions must be made and an educator needs an example of how your child thinks.

SPECIAL STRUGGLES

The label "gifted" can either hinder or help a child. You see, contrary to popular thought, being deemed gifted doesn't necessarily mean life is made easier. Even kids with recognized gifts—precisely *because* of those gifts—struggle with:

- conflicts with parents and siblings (who may wonder if they are less valuable without the same gifts)

- low self-esteem and perfectionism
- teachers who don't understand their needs or who try to teach using mismatched curriculum
- misunderstandings with peers
- difficult decisions regarding their future (with options limited by time and cost)
- undeserved pride and unwarranted shame (perhaps Mom or Dad struggle with this as well)

So what do you do if your child displays a remarkable talent of some sort—a gift that makes him stand apart and draws endless comments from strangers (including advice from acquaintances on how you should parent)?

When a child is intellectually gifted, he may appear to be greatly appreciated. The problem is, he may feel appreciated for the wrong things, then spend a lifetime trying to prove he has value apart from his gifts.

That is why, even if your child has been labeled gifted, I think it is wise to rarely, if ever, define your child that way verbally, even to him or her. When my son was in a gifted education program, the only time I ever called it that was when another parent was interested in the program and needed to know the name of it. Otherwise, I usually just said he was in accelerated classes. That may seem like semantic game-playing, but I really wanted to avoid having my son hear repeatedly that he is "gifted." His sister is also extremely bright yet isn't even interested in applying for the same program due to its rigor. Does that make her "ungifted"? Not in my eyes.

Once a gifted child is identified, he needs stimulating education and loving, supportive parents to meet his special needs. Author James Alvino said, "The cream doesn't always rise to the top; it sometimes sours and curdles."[2] A gifted child left to fend for himself probably won't reach his full potential.

[1] This checklist is based on information from the Council for Exceptional Children. If you answered yes to a few of these questions, keep your child's strengths in mind as you interact with him. Seek ways to keep him excited about learning. If you answered yes to many or most of these questions, an assessment by a school psychologist may help you determine what is best for your child academically.

[2] James Alvino, *Parents' Guide to Raising a Gifted Child* (New York: Ballantine, 1992).

FREE Discussion Guide for *Delight in Your Child's Design!*

A discussion guide written by Laurie Winslow Sargent

is available at

 ChristianBookGuides.com

Other Parenting Resources from Focus on the Family

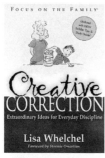

ISBN: 1-58997-128-0
$14.99

MORE FOR MOMS!

Creative Correction draws from Lisa's own successes and mistakes to help other parents deal with sibling rivalry, lying, and other behavioral challenges.

Her creative, down-to-earth encouragement and biblical perspective provide a breath of fresh air for overwhelmed parents everywhere.

ISBN: 1-58997-120-5
$12.99

DON'T LET THE MOMENT PASS YOU BY.

Learn how you can take advantage of ordinary, everyday experiences to grow your child's faith. *The Power of Teachable Moments* helps you discover how simple it really is to make God real in your child's life.

As the authors outline what those experiences are, how to recognize them, and what to do with them, you will be reassured by how natural these moments can be, and you will have more confidence to spiritually nurture your child.

ISBN: 1-58997-164-7
$8.99

IS THE SPEED OF LIFE BLURRING YOUR PARENTING?

Careers, errands, soccer games, chores, and friendships . . . whew! In the midst of such a frantic pace, parents often find it hard to effectively connect with their children.

Parenting at the Speed of Life offers 60 ingenious tips for using ordinary daily events to capture your kids' hearts.

$\mathcal{A}$lso Available by Laurie Winslow Sargent:

ISBN: 0-8423-5764-5
$16.97

TEACH VALUES, ENHANCE CONFIDENCE, AND REDUCE THE NEED TO DISCIPLINE— ALL BY HAVING FUN!

Do you ever feel too busy, too stressed, or simply too tired to play with your kids? Do you ever feel guilty because a game of Candy Land is *not* your idea of a good time?

Laurie Winslow Sargent explains that playfulness isn't measured by how many games or activities you do with your child; it's all about attitude.

The Power of Parent-Child Play is the first book to address many of the most common barriers to parent-child play: stress, boredom, personality conflicts, and lack of motivation. Inside you'll find lots of great ideas for overcoming those barriers and reaping the benefits of spending time with your kids.

Also includes:
• Activities and ideas for finding joy in your children
• Questions for reflection to help you apply these topics to your own family
• Resources and tools you can use to become a more playful parent

enjoy the **journey**™

Does parenting sometimes seem like an overwhelming task? Your role as a parent is difficult but very important to you and your children, and Focus on the Family® wants to encourage you! The complimentary Focus on Your Child® membership program has age-specific materials that provide timely encouragement, advice and information for today's busy parents. With newsletters or audio journals delivered straight to your doorstep once a month and a Web site packed with over 900 articles, Focus on Your Child can help you enjoy the journey!

Here's what the membership includes:

Parenting Newsletters: Four age-specific and concise editions for parents with no spare time.

Audio Journals: Timely information for parents and fun activities for children, based on their ages.

Online Resources: Age-customized articles, e-mail news, recommended resources and topic-organized forum through which parents can share with one another.

To sign up, go to www.focusonyourchild.com or call (800) A-FAMILY.